THE POWER TO BE YOU
42 BITES OF SELF-ESTEEM

Mariah Wolfe

Copyright 2018 Mariah Wolfe

CONTENTS

BITE 1
WHY A DO-IT-YOURSELF BOOK ON SELF-ESTEEM?

To me, healthy self-esteem is not only about affirmations. Affirmations can be used with success, but the absolute number one criteria for affirmations to be useful is that you believe in them – you can feel them in your stomach, not just in your thoughts. Without truly believing the words, they become not only unauthentic, but can feel offending and damaging regardless of who you are sharing them with.

I have been on the lookout for a book that deals specifically with self-esteem written in a language easily comprehensible to everyone. A book that could give tools to work with self-esteem in a forthright and honest way.

For twenty years I myself have been working with self-esteem both personally and professionally. The majority of people experience the challenges of working with self-esteem, so there's no shame in feeling overwhelmed by the challenges.

On the contrary making a decision to do something about it is, in my perspective, brave and energetic. Working with your self-esteem will change your life, offer you new opportunities and bring old patterns to an end.

The process can be hard and challenging since we – as human beings – take to the safe and well-known instead of seeking and doing what we know is best for us.

Some of my knowledge on self-esteem is presented in the book together with a host of exercises that have been tried out partly by myself and partly by those addressing me in my capacity of psychotherapist.

I know it works. However, I know too that you must really commit yourself wholeheartedly to the matter. Be patient with yourself recalling that "Rome was not built in a day". Realize your small successes in the process – then pat yourself on the back – it is important that you begin to become your own parent – the way your own parents ought to have been!

This is the point about working with self-esteem. You are to find your way home to yourself, realizing what will be right for you and offering yourself what others have not been capable of. Having realized this you will be capable of distinguishing between those who give you what you deserve and those who do not and must be avoided.

We were born with the capacity to adjust and develop – which is fortunate; what is not appropriate in our lives can most often be changed by our own influence.

In my practice I am often approached to explain self-esteem and to recommend books on the subject. I felt that most books on the subject were either too theoretical with not enough hands-on or simply too complicated to read. When I wanted to translate my book to English, I found out that a lot of the books in this language recommend affirmations and that some English speaking cultures have had quite a lot of challenges getting the method to work - simply because saying affirmations become mechanical and shallow. When they do, they can actually have the opposite effect on people.

I decided to write a book that dealt with self-esteem in a more accessible and to-the-point way and in my translation it became important to point out that real self-esteem does not come from only telling yourself, that you are ok - you have to believe it and feel it.

People are often quite surprised by the number of personal issues that can be attributed to low self-esteem. The good news is that everybody can improve her/his self-esteem without great difficulty once the process has actually been started.

We were all born with the ability to develop ourselves in many areas, including our self-esteem.

Low self-esteem may cause:

- ❖ A feeling of being "wrong"

- ❖ Stress

- ❖ Depression

- ❖ Drug / alcohol addiction

- ❖ A general feeling that life is without meaning

- ❖ Eating disorders

- ❖ Broken relationships

- ❖ Extreme shyness

❖ Lack of interest in eating, playing, exercising and sex

❖ Lack of courage to air your opinions

❖ Repetition of unsolved conflicts

❖ Feeling that nobody understands you

❖ A fear that other people may find you odd

❖ Feeling that you are stupid

❖ Being intensely concerned with other people's opinion of you

ANNIE;

"I just wasn't happy. I noticed that my sister, who had attended therapy, seemed to take greater joy in her everyday life. I decided to give it a try myself and start with your book. Although it was very difficult step to get started, my only regret is that I hadn't done it earlier in my life."

BITE 2
HOW TO USE THE BOOK

The opening chapters will help you gain some knowledge of the subject, some of which you might recognize from your own life and you will also gain some insight into why you behave a certain way in various situations.

Several exercises are to be found throughout the book, although the majority are collected in chapter # 10 :"Ways to Improve Your Low Self-esteem". You can choose to work with one or more exercises at a time, depending on your personal energy and strength. Take small steps until you get the hang of it.

You may skip straightaway to the exercises; however, developing your self-esteem can be an extensive process. Imagine the number of years that you have spent living with and nurturing your low self-esteem. It does require both time and effort to break these habits. Reading the book is an exercise in itself, so allow yourself all the time you need to take it in. People rarely improve straight away, most people develop in stages, so take the time you require and allow yourself one step at a time.

How old are you? Even if you do need a few years to properly improve your self-esteem, it will only represent a mere fraction of your entire life. It will be worth your while to read the book before, during and after you have begun practicing the exercises. It will also enable you to discuss the subject with yourself and others.

I recommend that you do yourself the favor of reading the book twice a year or more, as you might forget certain passages or exercises after a while.

Brushing up on it will do you good and may move you a step forward each time you read the book. Your decision to read the book again is in itself a victory because it proves to yourself that you are seriously dedicated to improving your self-esteem.

You may want to put a reminder in your calendar every three to six months to read the book and repeat the exercises. In that way you will continue the good work you have started.

You could compare yourself to a garden. The flowers grow and need pruning, watering, care and sun. If you leave the garden unattended for too long it will wither. Like your self-esteem the garden needs some tender care and attention on a regular basis.

Working with your self-esteem does take time, so start with one exercise. Once you are satisfied with the outcome of the first exercise, move on to the next and so on. Don't expect any results in your everyday life until you have successfully worked with a couple of exercises for a while. Be happy and content with the little changes you feel in yourself. Even the slightest change indicates that you are on the right track!

The reason, or reasons, for your low self-esteem will not disappear - they will always be a part of you and your personal history. You will, however, learn to relate to them and handle them so the consequences of your low self-esteem will no longer control your life. The more work you put in, the less you will be influenced by your low self-esteem and you will feel you yourself are in control of your life, having brought your unhealthy self-esteem under control.

Working your way yourself towards a healthier self-esteem can as I mentioned be hard. I recommend that you get together with others who are already in the process or who wish to improve their self-esteem. Share your progress and help each-other over the hurdles.

Therapy might be inevitable, if you find that you are so influenced by your low self-esteem that you find it hard to work with the exercises. Therapy can be supportive in the process and you might also speed up the process by having a professional person on the side-lines.

The book cannot replace therapy. The best way for a person to develop is in the company of other people – some might say it's the only way! During therapy sessions there are personal situations that cannot be described in a book. Being in therapy and working on your self-esteem will be completely different from reading a book where you are given some "working tools" and gain insight.

Regardless of whether you start working alone or in the company of others, it is important that you share your progress with others, both your successes and what you find hard. If you don't have or feel that you don't have someone in your life with whom you can share your personal development and difficulties, a psychotherapist or counselor may be a valuable asset to begin with. In the long run you will however need to form intimate relationships with other people - even if you have to start with a self-help group, as ACA, Al-Anon or ACON it's better than nothing. Hopefully you can come to feel safe sharing your inner thoughts and work your way from there. Don't be discouraged - you didn't get the proper tools to form relationships from your parents, so how you blame yourself? Instead, you can close your eyes and feel in your gut that you feel good doing this for yourself.

MARY:

"It was really hard for me to open up and speak my mind the first couple of times. But as I realized that nobody was mocking me, I stayed on and that made me stronger. I can't say that I have 100% confidence in myself by now, but it is quite a relief not hiding who I am."

Bite 3
Why Is Healthy Self-Esteem Of Great Importance?

Self-esteem is important in all aspects of life. To be happy you have to have an honest and supportive relationship with yourself. This is needed to have an honest relationship to others, no matter if they are co-workers, family or friends. Also conflicts between you and the people who mean something to you, can only be truly resolved if you are able to express your true self. (And you can only have conflicts with people who mean something to you)

If you can't express your true self, can't say what is on your mind and show who you are, it will be difficult for others to trust you, because they don't quite know where you stand. When others don't trust you, they will treat you accordingly which will influence your trust in yourself. And you will lose confidence in yourself.

On the other hand, low self-esteem will make you trust yourself less. When you don't have confidence in yourself, you can't know yourself and show others who you are, tell them what you want and what you stand for - a vicious circle is set in motion, your low self-esteem is being confirmed and maintained.

It turns into a "hen or egg" situation : Which came first? People's reactions to you, or your own low self-esteem? In this case there is no doubt; low self-esteem "decides" whom you mix with and how - and it keeps itself going in this way.

Self-esteem is what you are worth to yourself. You are the most important person to you. It doesn't mean you are worth more than others. Other people are most important to themselves as well – or they should be. Once you are aware of your own worth, it helps you to understand what others are worth as well.

If you get the feeling that you are more or less worthy than others you are being unfair to yourself and them.

Placing yourself on a pedestal will give you a feeling of loneliness as will the idea of being pitied. It keeps others at a distance if you treat them as if they are worth more or less than you.

That means loneliness will hit you as well.

BITE 4
DO YOU RECOGNIZE YOURSELF?

Every person has that little inner voice that tells him/her what is wrong and right in different situations. It is like a record being played over and over, and we don't even think of where it came from. We don't question whether it is reasonable or not - or what sets it off.

Here are some examples of what people with low self-esteem will tell themselves - do you recognize any of them?

You may mark the ones you recognize and then go back later on to see if you are more positive towards yourself.

- ❖ I am not going to say anything, what I have to say is of no importance.

- ❖ I keep to myself because the others don't mean anything to me. They probably won't understand me anyway.

- ❖ I'm sure it is my fault.

- ❖ I don't want to be a burden to others.

- ❖ I ought to know better.

- ❖ That was really stupid of me. I'll just behave as if nothing has happened.

- ❖ I don't know how to do this, never did. Even at school the teacher said I couldn't do it.

- ❖ Why should they want to talk to me?

- ❖ It is very difficult for me to stick to the resolutions I make; to lose weight, exercise, stop smoking or make other changes in my lifestyle.

- ❖ Say three good things about myself? I can't!

- ❖ I don't care about others. They are stupid, they don't understand me.

- ❖ It is everybody else's fault that I am having a hard time.

- ❖ My best isn't simply good enough. I´ll show them!

- ❖ I know everything and if you disagree, it just goes to show I am right.

- ❖ Never mind!

Self-esteem is not reserved for certain social classes of people. Low self-esteem is not limited to those who grew up under socially-poor circumstances, who are very quiet or very vocal.

Low self-esteem is more common than many people realize - it is practically ubiquitous in people in the western world - and more the rule than the exception

It is very easy to look at a person who behaves a bit differently than the average person, and then claim that s/he behaves as s/he does, because s/he suffers from having low self-esteem. It might be true but low self-esteem is not accompanied by a certain behavior. Low self-esteem can certainly explain it but cannot excuse a certain way of behavior. If a person is violent, we can possibly refer it to low self-esteem, but it is not an excuse and the behavior is still unacceptable.

Friendly, well-organized, efficient people can just as easily suffer from low self-esteem in one or more areas.

That is why we can't use low self-esteem as an excuse for people who are not friendly or supportive.

"Oh, well, that's just because he has a low self-esteem!", might work as an explanation, not as an excuse. Usually our behavior is more like a survival technique, which we were taught by the adults who dealt with us when we were children.

If a person is very quiet and self-effacing or arrogant and progressive, we might be able to explain it with low self-esteem. It often relates to a certain behavior seen in their parents - and children do adopt their role models´ way of dealing with life.

Some people thrive on being quiet, some thrive on being in the spotlight, but it does not mean that they suffer from low self-esteem.

However, there are some behaviours that relate directly to low self-esteem: anxiety, depression, fear of intimacy, fear of success, alcohol-, drug, - and food abuse, sexual problems and violent actions.

But, it is important to realize that in none of these cases, can low self-esteem be used as an excuse for not changing the circumstances.

RUTH:

"As a child I did all I could to satisfy the adults in my life. I I did not know what I was doing at the time. It didn't work either, nothing ever seemed to be good enough. I truly wish we had been taught about self-esteem at school."

BITE 5
EXAMPLES OF LOW SELF-ESTEEM

Having low self-esteem will make you to do things which, in hindsight, may seem rather strange, but at the time it seemed perfectly sensible. You were taught this behavior earlier in your life and it will keep you from having success, making new friends, having adventures, facing challenges and changes. It is simply a mental straitjacket, put on you by the adults in your childhood. As a grown-up you yourself maintain this mental straight jacket.

The adults of your childhood may never have spoken a word to cause your low self-esteem to grow. It may be the signals they sent you and the everyday life you led at the time.

Children always co-operate and sense much more than the spoken word. Let's look at some examples:

GERTIE'S STORY:

Gertie, 35 years old, feels uncomfortable in large crowds. When she attends parties or gatherings, she is sitting by herself and never talking with anyone.

During her educational years Gertie never participated in discussion groups or joined committees, which may both serve as sources of networking and of making friends for life.

Gertie says she does not approve of loud people, people who talk a lot, interrupt or in any way make themselves noticed. Gertie would like learn to accept people the way they are because she genuinely feels she is missing something.

We begin her therapy sessions by looking at her feelings for people who are not afraid of voicing their opinions or afraid of showing the world who they are. We dig a bit deeper and I ask her to look back to remember when her parents said or did anything to support that feeling. It appears that her parents have the same feelings as Gertie about loud people.

Gertie tells me of family gatherings when she was a child. Both her parents complained about the noise and behavior of the other children at the parties and how irritating it was when their parents couldn't control them.

Her mother had looked at her saying something like this, "We are so fortunate to have our little princess, she is so quiet and behaves herself". Then her mother had kissed her.

Gertie remembered the knot in her gut, but also an inner quiet joy from being praised by her mother.

As a child, Gertie was praised whenever she was quiet and unobtrusive. Gertie hardly ever played with the other children and every time she quietly played on her own she was highly praised. "What a clever little daughter we have, she knows how to amuse herself", Her parents had looked very proudly at her.

Gertie was craving for her parents' love and acceptance, children will always do that by default, so she made an effort to be quiet. As time went by, Gertie became afraid of engaging with the other children in the neighborhood, or joining their noisy games.

Gertie told me that she didn't have any memories of ever climbing trees, having a friendly fight, chasing each other on bikes or even participating in a snowball fight.

During therapy sessions, slowly but surely Gertie becomes aware that her opinion of other people's behavior really was not her own; it was that of her parents'. She realizes that this attitude controlled her entire childhood. Not because her parents wanted to control her, but because children will always try to cooperate.

She realizes that she has adopted this opinion of people around her and that it still controls her as an adult. Gertie feels a loss of wasted experiences and opportunities which she missed in earlier life and decides to change that.

It takes time and quite a lot of boundaries and artificial limits have to be crossed. But during the process Gertie makes new friends and has lots of new experiences. She says in her own words that she has become much more integrated.

Low self-esteem is always an impediment to our self-expression, and sometimes we are not even aware of what is at stake.

CASPER:

"My self-esteem was so unhealthy that I didn't find any joy in life. I wasn't interested in food. I only ate because I had to. I didn't have any friends because the adults of my childhood always gave me the distinct feeling of being wrong."

KEITH'S STORY:

Keith is a 21- year- old student. He has an exam coming up on a topic he doesn't care much about. Keith has been told by his teacher that he is not strong in that particular subject which is difficult for him. Keith studies all he can but somehow it just feels too difficult.

He hears an inner voice that keeps telling him it's too hard. He gets a rather unpleasant feeling every time he tries to study. He is constantly focusing on something else apart from studying and his thoughts keep sidetracking so it is difficult to remember the texts. He reads for an hour but in reality he hasn't read very much.

Now he feels how difficult it is for him, and it has to be since the teacher says he just isn't any good at it.

The unpleasant feeling keeps growing and he decides to postpone the studies until the next day. The result is the same.

Having fought for some weeks he feels extremely frustrated at being unsuccessful in preparing for the exam. He is angry with himself for his lack of ability and motivation; he throws the book aside and decides : "Never mind".

He feels stupid and lazy, and no matter what he does, he will not be ready for the exam. "I'll fail anyway, so why bother wasting any more time studying. I am not going to learn it anyway".

At the exam he fumbles and wishes frantically that it would be over and done with. He flunks which now confirms his own belief that he is no good.

Keith wants therapy because he has a hard time accepting that he is so "stupid" (in his own words). He needs help to accept that there are things he is not good at. Keith discovers that, among others, his teachers expressed the negative expectations of him. Instead of supporting him, he was branded as a child who didn't have the ability to learn. The teacher talked to his parents who out of concern tried to make him understand that he was to push himself on top of them pushing him.

Keith realizes that the idea of not being good at the subject was not his own originally but came from his former teachers, not himself. Not until he became an adult did it become his own idea. He actually enjoys the subject and wants to explore it.

He signs up for some subjects at adult education courses, telling the teacher how negative his feelings for the subject are. This turns out to be an entirely different experience for Keith. The earlier losses are regained; Keith passes the exam and he is truly proud and happy. Keith now has confidence in himself and his own abilities; he just has to listen to himself instead of listening to the "broken record" from his former teachers and his parents.

What appears to be laziness may turn out to be a symptom of low self-esteem.

When you have low self-esteem the feeling of never being quite good enough may be rather persistent. Your family loves you but you don't love yourself. You may be admired by your acquaintances but still feel worthless. You may win a prize but still feel you could have done much better. You may be confident and self-assured but still feel on shaky ground.

Ever since you were a child your surroundings branded you by treating you in a special way which also influenced your way of thinking of yourself.

SUE:

When Sue started therapy she felt a loser. "I have no backbone", she claimed. "The decisions I make are of no consequence. It seems as if I cannot complete anything.. All my dreams are broken and I shall never be able to lead a normal life".

During therapy Sue slowly began to look at herself in a different light. "Now I realize that my parents simply didn't have the ability to give me a healthy self-esteem. They both suffered from an unhealthy low self-esteem, they felt like losers on the lowest rung of the social ladder. They could not give me anything but that feeling. I still remember the feeling of not being good enough, feeling that I can't do anything right, I still have it but it's no longer the main feeling.

I look at myself differently today, I realize I have moved forward and that gives me the hope that I can move even further.

Sometimes when I don't succeed I tell myself, "I will try again and do it better. And I know I can." That gives me confidence and my life has now become an exciting process that allows me to realize that I am valuable and that my life is worth a lot."

Try to think about successful people. I don't mean people with financial success but people who feel great and are living the sort of life they want. Regardless of their jobs, postman or manager, the difference between them and people with low self-esteem is that they think positively of themselves. They look at life as an ongoing process, an exciting journey with challenges instead of the swamp of low self-esteem from which they cannot escape.

Like the duckling in Hans Christian Andersen's fairy tale "The Ugly Duckling" you can bow your head to watch your reflections in the water which reveal that you are a swan and not the Ugly Duckling. You can stop looking at yourself through other people's eyes. Look at yourself and the world around you through your own eyes.

It can be a rather lengthy and difficult process to change the way you look at yourself – and at others. Hopefully this book will be a helpful tool on your way to a healthy self-esteem.

Joe says,

I would have been much better off if I had begun therapy much earlier. But better late than never, now I am on my way to being quite happy with being the person I am.

BITE 6
THE FIRST EXERCISE - AFFIRMATIONS THAT WORK

Here's the first exercise. It deals with changing your way of thinking and of talking about yourself.

You'll have better results with this exercise if you do it every day. You have to think of the exercise as a daily ritual. Waking up in the morning you can think: "Today I will practice thinking of myself as someone with a higher self-esteem."

If you have moments during the day when you think: "I'm a loser, I have no backbone, I am no good, I am certainly not good enough " or something like that then make a mental note of it. When you find yourself having these thoughts, instead, start thinking: "I am on my way to become a human being worth loving, I'm good enough, I can do anything I want to."

Talking to yourself in this way you program yourself to think differently and more positively. In fact you become your own parent; a caring and supporting parent of the little hurt child within yourself. You get the chance to change your programming. Instead of going on listening to the old program about you being useless etc., you turn it upside down by putting trust in yourself.

When you tell yourself something positive for the first time, it may sound like a load of crap and you do not believe it. Just imagine that it is actually true! Close your eyes and feel your gut to recognize what it feels like if it is true.

Take your time to recognize your gut feeling, not the feeling in your head but in your gut. You may put one hand on your belly sensing what it feels like being a human being on its way to becoming worthy.

Once you have found this gut feeling, hold on to it! Practice feeling it several times a day. In the future when telling yourself positive things, place your hand on your belly and recall the good feeling.

Waking up in the morning, make a decision that you will do this – just for today. Waking up tomorrow morning you can make the same decision.

Don't praise yourself if you can't feel the praise. If you try to tell yourself "I am ok" and you can't feel what it's like to be ok, start smaller. You can't learn to cook by jumping into the hardest recipe you can find - it's doomed. So instead say for example "I support myself in working towards being ok". Or you can say: "I am allowed to be ambitious with my life". Feel that. You feeling the words is the difference between empty affirmations that do more damage to you and truly working with your self-esteem.

Your brain, which reacts to all kinds of impressions from your surroundings, will do its utmost to get you back into the old patterns. It will spoil your concentration, make you think that you will never succeed and that it is just a silly old trick that cannot improve your life. You have to recognize this defense mechanism we possess that will hold on to what we are familiar with. What we are familiar with is "safe" although it may not be the best for us. Unfortunately, we will often choose what seems safe, well-known and easy for us instead of what will be better for us. However, you are now prepared. Not making long term plans for your work with your self-esteem may be a good way of cheating your brain. Just take it one day at a time.

Imagine that you succeed in thinking positively of yourself just once today! What huge success that will be for you! You will feel wonderful! Don't forget to sing your praises whenever it happens. (And feel the joy while doing it)

Even the smallest success deserves celebration. Just imagine you're doing something that you never did before – it's definitely worth patting yourself on the back.

BITE 7
CAN I WORK ON THIS AT ALL?

You may worry that you aren't capable of working on this idea of self-esteem. You may take it for granted that you were born with low self-esteem. You may be worried that you have lost so much in your life that you cannot regain it.

It may come as a surprise to you, but you already have a high self-esteem, the only thing you have to do is to remember it, so you can live it. Someone planted ideas in your head - you might say that your upbringing was brainwash - and you are still carrying around these ideas, because no one else told you how to get your own ideas about who you are. Until now - you have an idea of what you want or don't want with your life and that's why you are reading this book.

Newborn babies and young children will express themselves a hundred percent clearly during the first period of their lives - When angry or hungry they will scream, they will cry when feeling sad, afraid or missing their mother, they will chuckle when happy.

Babies will openly express whether or not they like the way others treat them. Babies will show neither modesty nor politeness, they will not hide their true feelings in order not to hurt or be tiresome. Babies are what they are and feel what they feel at a given moment.

When you were a baby - you were like that. However, your surroundings taught you what they thought was more appropriate ways to express your needs – or they taught you to abstain from expressing them at all.

It goes without saying that it would be inappropriate to scream and cry when feeling something, however, basically you have to find the baby in you that expressed how it was without restrictions. Since you were like that once, you may come back to that again, but now with greater insight, experience and a will to choose when to use. It is a nice feeling, isn´t it?

THE WAY IN WHICH YOU REBUILD YOUR SELF-ESTEEM MAY REMIND YOU A LITTLE OF MUSCULAR TRAINING

A muscle can be trained since it is already there, although it is untrained. As you train it, it gets more and more visible.

Self-esteem is like a muscle that has to be kept up in order that it may stay visible. Training a muscle becomes a habit upon which you do not reflect. You find it pleasant and like the result. At some point you stop training to enjoy the result. Working with your self-esteem is the same.

You will reach a point when it becomes so natural for you to train your self-esteem that you will enjoy doing it and find pleasure in the result without further reflection.

BITE 8
WHAT IS SELF-ESTEEM?

Self-esteem cannot stand alone. We have all been provided with some basic parts in the core of our personality which are or are not stimulated in our early lives. Together with our attitude to emotions, these basic parts decide most of our grown-up relationships with the surrounding world, ourselves and other people. The very core is the part that is basically always yourself and that is where your self-esteem "lives".

The basis of how you react to other people will be found here.

If you are fully aware of yourself and aware that you are OK this will also form the basis of how you meet other people – and your reactions will follow this pattern.

Having a good core will make it much easier for you to interact in healthy ways with other people. You will then think and react in an appropriate way that gives you peace, strength and energy. The relationship with yourself must be well balanced in order that your relationship with others flourishes.

Your personality is made up of more parts, but, basically there are three areas to be focused upon when working with your self-esteem; namely self-feeling, self-esteem and self-confidence.

Just to give you an idea about the three concepts:

Self-feeling

Self-feeling means you can sense all your emotions – that is when you feel, anger, sadness, happiness, confusion or fear.

A well-developed self-feeling is necessary to have a good self-esteem.

Quite a number of people are taught as children not to sense their emotions, because emotions are unwanted parts of the personality according to their parents. Normally it is not conscious on the part of the parents, they were brought up in the same way and consequently they pass on an identical child rearing-method.

The parents may show that they dissociate themselves from certain emotions.

They may show their dissociation by placing the child in another room, when he is sad or shows anger or the child may be shouted at or even ignored. Parents may say things like:

"Big boys don't cry"

"Good girls must behave"

"Go to your room until you have can be good again"

Mostly this is about parents who find it difficult to handle their own emotions. They are so used to anger being a bad thing, so when they get angry at their child, they get angry with themselves at the same time because they got angry. Or one or both parents may be (unconsciously) afraid of what will happen if they lose control and, therefore, their anger is mixed with powerlessness which the child understands as "I don't know how to cope with you". Feelings of anger and grief will be rejected by grown-ups and that is why they are gradually suppressed in the child. Add to this that these emotions are heavy to carry for the child on its own.

When treated this way, children will stop showing these emotions except in extreme situations. The problem is that if a person cannot become really angry, it will follow that s/he can't feel real happiness either since all feelings are intertwined. If we suppress one emotion, the other emotions will be affected by that.

On a side note: A healthy reaction to your child's anger could be to look her in the eyes and say: "I can see that you are very angry. That's ok. Tell me if you need me to hold you while you're angry." If the child becomes so angry he starts hitting and kicking, pick him up gently and hold him as gently as you can while saying: "I am helping you to be angry without breaking things". If she starts hitting you, gently hold her arm and tell her: "I don't want you to hit me". Maybe you have to do this many times, but this is the way to show your child that it is ok to be angry, it's ok to show it, but it's not ok to break things or hit others. You yourself must be calm while doing it. You can only be calm, if you can contain yourself and your own emotions. If you can't, say so: "I get angry now, so I can't help you and be a good parent. I am sending you to your room. I am sorry.

This way you take responsibility for your emotions and actions, so the child is clearly told that it is not because there is something wrong with him.

To some parents a child's sadness will evoke a reaction that is so unbearable, embarrassing or frightening that parents tease or taunt the child when he is crying in order to make it stop.

That is how the child is taught to suppress his tears and sadness.

Sometimes only the child's anger is acceptable to her parents and then this may become the way the child expresses herself when she is actually sad.

On a side note: A healthy reaction to sadness in children is to do much the same as with anger. Look her in the eyes if you can and tell her: "I can see that you are very sad. It's ok to be sad." Pick her up gently and rock her from side to side without words. If the child reacts physically to you holding her by hitting or turning her back on you, you might say: "I can see that you are angry as well as sad." If the child is trying to get away from you, let it. You are not always what your child needs. But if she starts acting out, pick her up again and use the methods from when she is angry.

These methods help the child put words on her emotions, shows her that you can contain her emotions and that you take responsibility as an adult. It may be really hard for you to do these things at first because you are not yourself brought up to deal with emotions in a healthy way. That's ok - you are not a bad person for missing these skills - and you can get them!

The child of another family may learn to be silent and reserved if his parents neither like weeping nor angry children. Children want to cooperate and will often give the parents what they are asking for, directly or indirectly.

Can you feel when you are sad or angry? Not the following day, or even a few hours later, but right when it is happening - and do you know if it is sadness or anger you are feeling ? In that case you possess self-feeling.

This also applies to happiness! Sensing your emotions is one step toward repairing your self-esteem.

John says,

It puzzles me why children are not taught self-esteem at school in our country. In the long run it would save a lot of money if children grew up to become human beings that would take themselves and others seriously.

Self-esteem

Self-esteem means that you know that you are 100% ok – that is you know that you are a good human being doing your best who deserves to be loved and respected in return simply because you are you.

Although we have never met, I know that the above applies to you – for it applies to every human being.

But this doesn't mean that it's ok to do things that will harm or hurt others. And it doesn't mean that others can't be angry with you or hurt if you harm them.

Possessing healthy self-esteem makes it much more difficult for you to be thrown you off balance since you don't depend on what others mean, think or say about you. You know that you are good enough (not necessarily better than others or the best, simply good ENOUGH) regardless of what happens and you can consequently deal with defeat and hard times.

Regardless of what happens, it does not shake the picture of you as someone valuable and good. In this way you become governed by your own inner feeling of value – governed by something inside you instead of something outside.

We are all good enough, have always been and will always be. However, you can easily feel that you are not ok if in childhood and later in adult life you were repeatedly rejected because of actions, feelings and remarks.

We are not automatically equipped with the power to reveal and fix this, so we grow up with an unconscious sense of guilt feeling that we are not good enough.

Do you deserve to meet all embracing love without having to do anything for it? To many people unconditional love does exist – outside of books or movies.

Unconditional love does not mean your partner has to accept any inappropriate acts on your part, if you behave violently, let your partner down or in any other way show acts of self-hatred that will affect your partner or others.

If you hit your partner, you still deserve to be loved, but your action is not ok – there is a distinction between actions and personality. You are the only one who can change your actions, the person who loves you cannot do that. The consequence may be that they have to move away from you physically until you have changed your actions.

Marie says, I didn't get enough attention from my husband. He was always too busy, job was more important and he simply didn't understand me. I blamed him for making me miserable. In therapy I learned to let go of this idea and understand that he might be unable to give me what I wanted, but so was I and in the end I could not change him, but only me. I learned to give myself what I needed, so I was not dependent on a man to give it to me. When I learned this, I met a guy who was able and willing to give me what I needed. Now I could enjoy getting attention from him, but I was not dependent on it. That really freed me.

We consist of what we are, what we have and what we do. What we do and what we have might change, but who we are will never change. It is the beautiful living being you are with all your qualities and emotions.

Self-confidence

Possessing self-confidence means that you dare show what you can do and use your abilities to pursue your dreams. For example, you draw on your self-confidence when you are going to make a speech or when you have an important job interview or you are working on a project that you believe in.

Do you dare to join in a discussion among a crowd of people you are not familiar with? If so you have probably a high self-confidence.

It is quite common to possess self-confidence without having self-esteem, however, it is rare that the opposite is the case – I have not yet come across it. Possessing self-feeling forms the basis of self-esteem and with self-esteem comes self-confidence as well.

SELF-FEELING: you are capable of sensing your emotions when they are present.

SELF-ESTEEM: you feel and know you are worth loving.

SELF-CONFIDENCE: you dare to use your skills and abilities.

BITE 9

WHAT ADVANTAGES CAN HEALTHY SELF-ESTEEM GIVE YOU?

You can make an effort to improve your self-feeling, doing so you will automatically improve the two other elements, self-confidence and self-esteem – and this is one of the reasons for the above definition of the three concepts. Practicing your self-feeling is one of the ways of raising your self-esteem – taking yourself seriously by showing the surrounding world that you have the courage of your convictions is another.

If you happen to feel hurt by something someone says to you, the exercise will be to sense what it feels like to be hurt. And then you tell your counterpart what you feel like, which may be done where you can talk without being disturbed, saying for example, "It hurts my feelings when you comment on my dress."

Now you are being assertive.

Having the courage of your convictions will make you see that others too begin to take you seriously and expect honesty on your part in return both privately and at your job. Nobody says it is going to be easy – it will demand a lot of practice but it can be done and it is worth the effort.

Most of us live our lives with a feeling of low self-esteem to some degree. You may always sense a touch of it, however, you can reach a point when it no longer affects you very much. Even a slight improvement may result in success and make you acquire a taste for keeping up your work with your self-esteem. Maybe the very fact of knowing that you're not the only person with low self-esteem could raise your self-esteem? You are not alone!

Your self-esteem – either high or low – influences your working life, relationships and ambitions in life. When you start working with it, it may result in difficulties for both yourself and the people around you. You may do or say things that are unusual for you or not expected from you.

Therefore, it may be a good idea to let the people around you know that they can expect changes and ask them to support you in the way you may want. They may not want to or be able to do so, but, it is important that they know what you are expecting from them. And similarly, it is important that you know whom you can count on when the going gets tough.

That will make your task easier for you.

Martin says,

I was the kind of guy in control of everything-publicly. In reality it was only a facade and when it started developing cracks I had nothing to fall back on. It resulted in a long, painful process to find my way back to what really matters in my life."

Here's a list of some of the changes you may encounter while striving to achieve higher self-esteem.

Now try to tick off the items you would like to experience:

- You can back yourself up to a much higher degree.

- You can stand up to other people but also tell others when something makes you happy.

- Your confidence in others becomes strengthened.

- Your self-confidence will increase.

- You become happier – about yourself and about your life.

- You can cope with all the different people you come across on your way without making their problems your problems.

- You will stop believing that other people are out to get you.

- You will realize that everybody is doing his/her best, even though it may not always be enough.

- You will realize that other people don't automatically think badly of you – on the contrary.

- You will allow your dreams to come true.

- You dare to be yourself, although other people want you to be someone different.

- You can find a partner – and remain in the partnership without giving up your own personality.

- You hear what is actually being said, instead of trying to interpret the meaning of it.

- You ask when you are in doubt.

- You may ask for help without feeling inadequate.

- You are in a better position to enjoy all the positive and wonderful things in life.

- You stop doubting all the time that you are doing well enough.

- The people around you have confidence in what you say because they know you always speak your mind.

- You can bring up your children so they have the opportunity to achieve higher self-esteem.

- You can choose the people who give you what you are in need of and choose to do without those whom you find destructive to your way of life.

- You can cope with your own feelings and those of others, without becoming frightened.

What used to be safe and well-known will always pull you back, tempting you to stop your personal development and accept the current state of affairs, although you're fully aware that this isn't the best for you.

Reading this book may mean that you decided, once and for all, that things can be different. As you can see from the previous examples, the reward is noteworthy. In order to keep your habits from interfering with your development you can complete this process step by step with breaks in between.

You may feel tempted to sit down in the sofa, enjoying a piece of cake instead of practicing your self-esteem. You may be angry with yourself and think things like: "Why bother! It is too hard. I can't work it out!"

You have to break this pattern.

Allow yourself the time it takes, be patient and do the work step by step. Allow for breaks, praising yourself every time you have accomplished something hard. If you run into feelings like the above, ask yourself: "Is there one little thing or exercise I could do to practise higher self-esteem before I sit on the sofa?" Then do that and then sit in the sofa!

BITE 10
HOW DO WE ACQUIRE LOW SELF-ESTEEM?

Self-esteem may change throughout your life.

A child, stimulated and loved throughout her childhood, may experience something traumatic that may result in the loss of trust in herself or even in others too. The person acquire low self-esteem, he or she may even get depressed, may even lose the will to live.

A child who, during childhood, experienced refusals, violence, severe scolding, abuse and neglect may as a grown-up choose to work with these episodes.

By doing so, you can gain higher self-esteem and in addition a better understanding of when your low self-esteem is at work. You may then counteract its impact in order to reduce its influence and make it less destructive.

JOHN'S STORY:

John grew up a cheerful boy in a happy and safe family. At school he was happy and industrious.

When John was 12 years old, his parents were tragically killed in a car accident, his younger brother was placed with a foster family, and John went to live with his grandparents. His grandparents lived close to his school so he walked to and from school instead of going by bus. However, several times from when he was 12 till he was 16, he was dragged into a gateway on his way to school and sexually abused while the perpetrator threatened to kill his grandparents, if he told anyone. John dared not say a word, but reacted violently by developing severe mood swings, becoming reserved, aggressive, and gradually losing interest in his school work.

His grandparents assumed that he was mourning the loss of his parents and he never told them anything. However, it upset him to such a degree that he lost faith in what is good others, behaving more and more angrily and aggressively.

Since he wasn't able to tell anyone what was wrong, the grown-ups in John´s life were powerless and at some point they lost patience. He was branded a problem child.

His misgivings assured him that he deserved what was happening to him - he did not deserve any better.

It was a long and tough process for John to regain his life as an adult. He never told anyone about the sexual assaults until he saw a therapist, and he struggled with feelings of desertion, loneliness, powerlessness and shame. Being afraid of other people's opinion of him, he withdrew from them. At the same time he wanted to cope with the trauma inflicted on him by the sexual assaults.

Slowly he opened up to the difficult feelings, and realized that he was not to blame for what happened. He worked his way through anger, sorrow and shame and began to realize that he was worth something. This changed his life.

LEA AND ANN'S STORY:

Lea is four years old and lives with her mother, Ann, who is 35 years old. Ann is self-employed, running her own web-based business. Lea is at home most of the time with her mother, because Ann believes it is the best thing to do since she has the opportunity. Being bored, Lea wants her mother to play with her, talk to her or show her mother the drawings she is making. However, Ann does not have time, very often she says, "Not now sweetie, I'm working!" "Please wait for mom to finish, this is important!" and "Please be quiet, I am going to make a phone call!"

Ann doesn't realize that she is rejecting Lea, who gets the feeling that she is unwanted. Why can't she be in preschool where they have so much fun?

Lea realizes that there are many things in her mother's life that are more important than Lea and gradually Lea withdraws from her mother's company, engaging in activities that don't bother her mother. She plays quietly with her dolls, talking to her fantasy friends who tell her that she must try to understand that there are more important things than her, and who comfort her when she is sad.

Lea wonders if she has done anything wrong since her mom doesn't want to be with her.

Ann sees a therapist because she has difficulties fighting her way through, believing that her business will be successful. She thinks that it may be because her mother was an alcoholic, but she is uncertain how it all adds up. During therapy Ann realizes that her mother would often drink on her own or in the company of other adults instead of caring for her daughter.

This is one of the reasons why Ann chose — unconsciously — to have Lea so much at home, however, she discovers she behaves like her own mother in rejecting and downgrading her daughter.

She decides that Lea is going to preschool and when she's home in the afternoon, the focus must be on Lea. Shortly after the changes, Ann experiences that Lea blooms and becomes happier and less clingy.

MINNIE AND PAUL'S STORY:

Minnie and Paul have a very strict father. It's very important to him that his children behave and make a good impression on other people in order that he may be proud. Proud of them and of their effort to become competent and respected citizens.

Therefore he makes schedules for them to follow when they come home from school and until bedtime. Do their homework, tidy up, clear the table, empty the garbage, make the beds and so on.

If Minnie and Paul do not fulfill all the items on the schedules, their father gets extremely angry. He will yell at them, calling them useless children that ought to be ashamed of themselves and that they have made him feel ashamed of them as well.

In order to practice their vocabulary and increase their intelligence, their father makes them do exercises in which they have to pronounce difficult words or explain difficult concepts.

By placing a huge pressure on them far beyond what would be reasonable according to their abilities and age he makes them feel stupid and incompetent.

If they do well, they may get money to buy little treats, but woe betide them if they spend all the money on themselves. Their father expects them to save up. They are not quite sure why he wants them to save money, but they do it. Partly because they want to be loved and accepted by their father and partly because they are deadly afraid of his temper.

Minnie, who suffers from low self-esteem as a grown-up, sees a therapist, realizing that she — as an adult - is still governed by her father's strict upbringing. She wants to break free of the fear of not pleasing him.

Do you remember what it felt like when the adults around you were not satisfied with you or didn't notice you? Were you noticed when you needed them? Or did they know or did they ask what you wanted?

What is characteristic of the above three examples and perhaps of the examples from your own childhood is that the child is neither heard, seen nor included.

BITE 11
SELF-ESTEEM IN THE UPBRINGING

Bringing up a child is walking a tightrope. On one hand you're teaching the child the norms and rules necessary to live in society. On the other hand you're helping the child to develop her own personality based on curiosity, happiness and self-knowledge.

It is natural for a child to develop in relation to the adults surrounding him and slowly but surely adapt to the society and the culture which he is to be part of.

This is not a conscious act at all, however, children will always choose the "wisest" behavior; the behavior which will give them the biggest social acceptance in their surroundings, or the behavior which will bring them the most attention.

If a child is told not to hit others, this will automatically become part of her inner set of rules. Let us suppose that what is unconscious becomes a conscious conversation with ourselves, it may run like this. "If I hit someone, I won't be ok, so I won't do that, since it's important that the others find me ok."

If the child is told not to hit others, but experiences that adults do so, the child will remember and try to figure out when it pays to hit others. "How can I gain what my father gained by hitting others, this is clearly something I am destined to gain" – an unconscious process that can only be stopped if the child is heard, seen and respected.

A child who experiences adults hitting is more likely to choose a violent partner or become violent themselves. It is a well known fact that this happens although the person is well aware that it is not the best choice, but with the familiar will often come a feeling of safety, although it is a somewhat far-fetched safety. It feels "safe" as in well-known, because if you grew up in a violent home, you know how to act around violent people. This means that when you look for relations in your life you will unconsciously look for someone who can make it possible for you to act the way you know.

Some might say: "I did not choose a violent partner!" No - but if you stay, you are choosing that partner - for every day that you stay you are choosing to be abused. Things are not black and white, but we are made to seek what gives us the comfort of patterns and actions we know how to relate to. This is also why it can be so hard to leave an abusing partner - in some ways it feels so safe and nice, because you always know what you get - even when it makes you unhappy. And whatever crumbs of love you get, you have learned to appreciate - this can be the reason why it is hard to accept relationships where you get a lot of love.

When a child is being heard, seen and respected and in this way experiences that adults do what they say, the child will choose not to hit others: "I can gain what I want without hitting anybody and it gives me a stronger feeling of being ok, so I go for that."

The child will feel he is heard when the adults take time to actually listen to what the child has to say, answering in words that truly show the child that every word was heard. Being seen means acknowledgement of the child's being instead of praise of the child's actions.

Another example comes from watching a child playing on a slide on the playground; the child is sliding down, shouting at her mother, "Just watch me, Mom! " Instead of saying, "Indeed, you are good at sliding", the mother replies, "I see you are having a great time". In this way the mother acknowledges the child's ability to enjoy the fun, rather than commenting on the child's "skill at sliding". This way the parent empowers the child to use the skills that make it feel good more than the skills that make the child feel accepted.

It is not wrong to praise your child when it is good at something. We all like to be good at something. The point is to be aware to empower the child's ability to make itself feel good to a much higher degree. You can choose where you want the child to be good at something and where you want your child to feel good

In order to feel respected the child must be encouraged to make certain decisions. The mother may ask, "Do you want to go out to play or do you want to play inside? It's your decision!" The child is given clear options and a feeling of making decisions on subjects of importance to her. Asking "What do you want to do today?" may be too vague and may be a conflict starter as the child might answer something that is beyond your limits, money or energy. Some parents have no problems on this issue, but if you have, try narrowing down what choices the child has..

As mentioned above, throughout our lives, we are programmed by means of the experiences we have. We learn to interpret situations and other people in certain ways. You may have learned unintentionally that violence forms part of love in a relationship.

Although your rational mind will tell you that it's unhealthy and wrong, your programming will tell you something different. Your "programming" will inform you that what is familiar is safest and if you are not fully aware of it you will automatically act according to your programming.

If your parents were not able to raise your self-esteem you will become more susceptible to outside influences. Low self-esteem may be caused by teasing at school or by teachers´ criticism.

It creates a vicious circle – the lower the self-esteem you possess the more susceptible you are to outside influences. The more susceptible you are the more you will misunderstand and misinterpret the signals from people around you, taking the signals to be personal criticism, leaving a feeling of not being good enough within you and lowering your self-esteem accordingly.

Every culture and family has its own ideas of what a child must be and attain to become a healthy and complete human being.

That is why we run into disagreements, we have various attitudes to life and the surrounding world but they can differ from person to person. And if we cannot stand disagreeing, conflicts will arise – we'll quarrel, attack each other and defend ourselves.

Are you listening to what others say? Or do you hear what you think they are saying? If your self-esteem is low, you are more likely to interpret what others are saying, and relate to it, instead of actually listening to what is being said.

All parents do their best. Therefore, it can be very frustrating knowing that episodes will probably occur that the child – as a grown-up - will look back on in sadness or anger regardless of what you did, although you did your best as a parent to further the self-esteem of your child and give him a good foundation in life. These can be minor episodes or major ones. Of course parents want their children to do well in life – to be able to create the life they want to live.

The best thing you can do for your children in order to further their self-esteem is to raise your own. In this way you show them the positive idea of wanting something better for yourself. And then, of course, talk with them about it, to make it acceptable talking about dissatisfaction, sorrow, anger, happiness and fear. If you can recognize and validate your children's feelings, you show them how they can recognize and validate their own and those of other people.

You must be able to recognize and validate your own feelings before you can accurately interpret those of others.

It may be difficult for you to deal with the anger or sadness of your own children if you, as a child, were not allowed to be angry or sad. You may reject them by telling them to go to their room, bribe them with candy or food or try to make their feelings go away: "Now stop crying, wipe your eyes, everything will be alright!"

Without being conscious of it we show our children in numerous ways how to react. A child may ask his parent, "Aren't you looking forward to the school play?" and the parent answers, "Of course I am!" However, the parent's body language signifies something totally different, namely, that the parent is lying, trying to hide the fact that the school play is not a particularly interesting event.

There may be many quite acceptable reasons for your reaction in this case or in similar ones, and you may not cope well with the task of telling your children the reason. However, the child is taught to hide its honest opinion from others and that is preferable to a difficult, but open dialogue. But a dialogue is always preferable, since children have an innate "syndrome of guilt" causing them to blame themselves for everything unpleasant. Thus, the child may think, "I may not perform well enough in the school play since they are not looking forward to it!" And this deprives the child of the opportunity to show others what he can do and build his self-confidence.

Here's another common example:

Mother, father and Joe are in line at burger place. Joe is a bit tired and impatient and it is crowded and noisy. Father says, "You just go and sit down and I shall bring you the food!" Mother looks at Joe and asks him, " Do you want to go and sit down?" Joe says "No", but Mother looks away, turns and walks away from the counter towards the table.

Thus Joe learns that, although grown-ups ask questions, they don't want to hear his answer. In other words they don't care about his opinion. It leaves him with the choice of making himself heard by reacting loudly and physically and hoping that his answer will then be respected or he may choose to become very quiet and apathetic – for it is of no use anyway.

You may unconsciously be asking questions of both grown-ups and children although you are not interested in the answers, even when the question is: "Do you love me?" or "Does my butt look too big in theses jeans?" If you do not want to hear the answer then stop asking! Find out what you really need and ask for that instead.

It is so much easier to get what you need if you ask for it directly. This feels better than if you tell others what you do not want or if you expect them to read your mind.

Children learn much more from what we do not say than from what we do say. Body language, actions and words have to be in accordance to make us reliable parents. Only by knowing yourself, daring to feel what is going on, being able to or wanting to put it into words may bring your body language, your actions and your words in accordance. You don't have to use five hundred words, just one or two sentences can let the child know that it is not the child who is to blame for a given situation.

In the example with the school play the mother might have answered, "You know, Mum is feeling a bit sad at the moment, so it is a bit hard to look forward to it today. But when we are there, I'll be very happy to see you play since I know you have had such a good time rehearsing".

If the child asks, "But why, Mum, are you sad?" the mother may reply," It is a bit difficult to explain, but it has nothing to do with you. I am not sad because of anything that has to do with you. You are not to blame!" This lets the child know that what Mum is feeling isn't his fault, and that there is nothing wrong with him looking forward to being in the play.

Children experience parents lying all the time:

At the dinner table father talks about his contempt for a neighbor, however, the following day he praises and flatters the neighbor when he sees him outside. Mother preaches honesty to the child, but lies to other grown-ups and to herself. Father and mother are quarrelling but protesting at the same time that everything is fine. On her job mother feels unappreciated and overworked, however, she suppresses her feelings because "she doesn't want to create any problems."

From this comes one clear signal: As a grown-up lying is accepted as a means of communication. Belonging is more important than being truthful.

This creates a society full of alienated individuals neglecting themselves and succumbing by the hundreds to stress and depression. A society in which people are not able to talk to each other about what's going on inside them; even though doing so would get some of their worries off their chests, and would make them feel accepted for who they are. A society in which you are afraid of being discharged or divorced if you speak your mind. A society where you visit a stress coach, buy hot stone massage treatments, receive tips on self-esteem on your Iphone – not as a supplement to a normally good life, but as a means of extinguishing small fires but only postponing the inevitable conflagration.

We deserve better.

It is really important not to blame our low self-esteem on our parents or on other grown-ups in our lives who were not perfect. Their actions may have caused your low self-esteem. However, by now you have become a grown-up, being capable of deciding to create your own life, not sticking to the patterns of your childhood home.

In other words - it is your choice.

BITE 12
BLAME AND SHAME

The use of blame and shame forms a natural part of bringing up children in our culture. Let us face it straight away – living without blame and shame is not possible, but some feelings of blame and shame are more appropriate than others.

You are not to "blame" for the origin of your low self-esteem and that is why you need not be ashamed of it. However, now you owe it to yourself to go ahead and repair it.

Kenn

Seven-year old Kenn steals money from his mother's purse, because she doesn't want to buy him an ice-cream. Now he plans to go down and buy it himself. But it is as if his gut turns into a big knot when he grabs a $5 bill, and a wave of shame washes over him.

Words fail him and the money feels very unpleasant. He knows it is wrong and inside him the conflict is boiling; the need for an ice-cream conflicts with cheating his mother. He knows it is wrong, but he feels so much like having an ice-cream. The money is burning in his hand and he feels the weight and tension in his body.

His whole body almost doubles up round the bill so that no one discovers his theft. Entering the ice-cream shop he looks around and the woman asks, "What do you want?" Kenn is feeling that she watches him as if she knows that he stole the money from his mother's purse. He thinks that she may be able to tell that he's a thief just by looking at him.

At long last he hands over a very sweaty $5 bill, orders his ice-cream and receives it. But walking into the sunshine to enjoy his ice-cream he feels very very guilty. It does not taste as good as he hoped, he eats it quickly and he walks home shamefacedly.

Mother is waiting at home and she catches sight of the ice-cream stains on his face and shirt. She asks him whether he has had an ice-cream and where he got the money for it and the knot in his gut explodes. Much ashamed, he breaks down crying and telling her that he stole the money for the ice-cream from her purse.

Doing something that he is well aware that grown-ups do not want him to do, Kenn feels blame and shame in the above example. He knows that he is to blame and he is consequently ashamed — and the discomfort he feels accompanied by his mother's anger may have a deterrent effect on him so he will not steal again. He was taught a lesson of great value.

BITE 13
BLAME AND SHAME IN THE UPBRINGING OF CHILDREN

Blame and shame constitute very strong weapons in the upbringing of children and ought to be used with caution. Used wrongly or in the extreme they may cause the child a permanent feeling of blame and shame, creating low self-esteem.

Certain expressions may contain elements of blame and shame which we convey to the child without taking into consideration what we are doing.

"We're going to see Aunt Ruth, you know, we owe her that". The underlying message is that actually we do not want to go see her, but we feel we owe it to her. The child is taught that we must do things because we owe it to someone, not because we want to do them.

The signal to the child would have been better if the grown-up had said and meant, "Aunt Ruth will be delighted to see us. It is nice to make her happy and that makes me happy too."

Another example: "You have to sit quietly, you owe me that. Otherwise you are not allowed to come with me on another visit". What the grown-up is telling the child is that nothing is free. The grown-up didn't bring the child for the fun of it, but because it is part of a deal and the child is to fulfill some expectations in order to be allowed to be together with the grown-up.

It would have been a better signal to the child if the grown-up had said," I know very well that it is very difficult to sit quietly, but I'll be happy if you try with all your might." The first part of the utterance contains the recognition that sitting quietly is difficult in order that the child doesn't feel shame, and the second part does not contain any threats of the consequences of not sitting quietly.

Using shame to make children behave: "Aren't you ashamed of yourself! Imagine that a girl your age wets her pants! Such a big girl behaving like a baby!" Not only was the child in this example physically unable to contain herself, but on top of the discomfort of having wet pants, she was told that she must be ashamed of herself. Now she gets the message that wetting one's pants is not only wrong, but is also an indication of not being able to act her age. The child in this case wasn't even aware of the expectation that she be able to avoid wetting her pants.

If the expectations are not fulfilled they will be used against the child. It would have been a better signal to the child had the grown-up said, "Oh, that's ok, wetting your pants is so unpleasant, I did that when I was your age. Let's go and change into something dry." By telling the child about herself wetting her pants, the grown up demonstrates to the child that she understands what the child is going through.

In this way it becomes easier for the child to deal with the fact that she wet her pants, since she is no longer the only one to do so. No big fuss is made of it, but the grown-up creates a kind of alliance by indicating that it is something the grown-up and the child can manage together.

Now try to close your eyes to sense what feeling guilty is like as if you did something wrong, try to feel what it is like being ashamed of something you did. You remember the feelings? You can recall them?

They are not very pleasant feelings and if a child is exposed to them to a great extent the reaction may be so overwhelming that the child cuts off the feelings. Once they have been cut off some work will have to be done to make them emerge again. Try the following exercise: try to remember situations as early as possible in your life when you felt shame and were to blame. Write down all the situations and write down what made you feel ashamed.

Then write down what you find appropriate and inappropriate today. don't use your parents´ yardstick, only your own, when deciding what is reasonable. You do not owe it to your parents to carry on their bad habits.

BITE 14
VARIOUS METHODS OF DEFENSE MECHANISM AGAINST EMOTIONS

Many people grew up in homes where certain feelings were not welcome. As a result you may have had to stow away your feelings, neither showing them nor feeling them. You may even have become so good at stowing them away that your body created some kind of defense against sensing them.

Since the child knows by instinct that revealing these feelings will result in negative experiences, all its efforts are — of course unconsciously - concentrated on avoiding contact with these feelings. It will continue to be so unless you as a grown-up decide to open up to them either during therapy or otherwise.

The defense mechanism which the child created unconsciously against these unwelcome feelings remains in the body and the body "remembers" them, activating them whenever the feelings are about to surface.

There are many different defense mechanisms: Some men have difficulties feeling and showing sorrow and sadness, and their defense mechanism is to get angry if something troubles them. Similarly some women have difficulties feeling and showing anger and they become sad or moody instead.

Tiredness, confusion and humor may be used as defense mechanisms. Here are a few examples of defense mechanisms:

Liz and Max´s Story:

Liz wants to have a talk with Max about their relationship. She is not satisfied with a few issues which she wants to be changed. Whenever she tries, Max fools around making jokes about what Liz is saying. He tries to make her laugh by mocking her attempt at starting a conversation about the way their relationship works. He makes fun of her, of the way she talks and the very topic of the conversation.

During their couples therapy Max becomes fully aware of what he is doing and wants to get to know the feelings lying behind his defense mechanism. he realizes his strong fear of losing Liz. His unconscious conclusion was that as long as he avoids discussing their relationship it will just go on the way it has been.

Sue´s Story:

Sue attends therapy because she succumbed to stress. Quickly she realizes that she has to become better at drawing the line at what she will stand.

But exploring her anger and practising to use it better to put people in their place who overstep her limits, confuses her. She cannot feel her anger, she cannot give it words. Both her words and her facial expressions signal confusion when she is asked to feel or express anger.

She starts to realize how confused she is, neither knowing what anger is nor how to make use of it without hurting others. She is bewildered at being unable to tell what's going on in her own body. Through simple breathing exercises and quiet Sue gets in contact with first her sorrow and then her anger.

BITE 15
GET IN TOUCH WITH YOUR OWN FEELINGS

You may get in touch with your own defense mechanisms when you try to get in touch with your own feelings. Emotions are based in your body so you feel them in your body, not in your mind.

Make yourself comfortable either by sitting down or lying down, close your eyes and call up the intense feeling of complete happiness. Think of an episode of great joy that would make you smile all over your face and make your body prickle. Try to get in touch with the joy in your body, hold on to it, get up and express it through cheering, dancing or some other physical activity.

Now try to do the same with anger. Think of a possible recent episode that made you furious or irritated. Recall it and feel the irritation and anger. Feel where it is located in your body and how and show your anger with your body. You may howl, beat on a pillow or do something else.

Now do the same with sorrow. Recall the sorrow and feel the deepest sorrow you have. Find it in your body and let it be expressed. You may sob, or curl your body in a foetal position, you may weep loudly calling for your mother – or something completely different.

It is a good idea to save a bit of energy the first times you practice – howling, kicking, laughing or dancing may be somewhat barrier-breaking if you are not used to it. Starting small and practicing over time will allow you to become more physical at your own pace.

Feeling silly when you practice getting in touch with your feelings? That would be a defense mechanism! Getting tired? That would be a defense mechanism! Are you being distracted from the exercise? That would be a defense mechanism!

Try to write down which defense mechanism you are using to avoid getting in touch with your own feelings. Since you now recognize your defense mechanism you may try the exercise again. Get in touch with the different feelings. If your defense mechanism raises its head you can recognize it and ignore it.

Try to write down, too, how feelings were looked upon in your childhood home – how did your father and mother react when you were very happy, angry or sad? How did your parents manage their own feelings? How they told you to handle your feelings is one thing, realizing how they acted as role models is something else to be aware of.

It might have been fine if you were weeping or feeling sad as a child, but if your parents never showed their own sorrow, it caused you to understand that showing your sorrow is ok for a child, but not for a grown-up.

Revealing your emotions might have been dangerous or forbidden when you were a child, but now you are the adult and you are the one to decide what is dangerous and forbidden. And none of your feelings can ruin you, break you down or change you into something worse than you are today.

A really joyful dance, a vehement burst of anger or an outburst of weeping is as healthy as good sex. By the way sex becomes better if you make good friends with your body and the feelings resting in it, and finding out that submission to emotions is not dangerous will put you in a better position to indulge in sex.

If you are afraid of your own anger and of your reactions when angry, it is even more valuable to do these exercises. You get in better touch with your emotions when you practise feeling them at their most powerful and you can turn them up and down to a higher extent when together with others.

Go ahead and practice getting in touch with your feelings pretty often. Where in your body can they be felt? Where do you find the feeling? How does your body react to that feeling?

It might help you to give words to the feeling by simply saying "I'm so happy", I'm so angry" or "I feel so sad" – try to say the words so you actually sound happy, angry or sad.

The more you practice the more feelings you get in touch with when they occur during everyday life. Tell yourself what happens for example "Whoops, I got angry with my colleague, and I can feel how I tightened my shoulders in the same way as when I practice at home".

As you become familiar with your feelings you can communicate effectively with your colleague - as in this example: "The fact that you took it for granted that I would stay late made me angry at you. I will stay this time, but I'd like to ask you not to take my willingness for granted, because that is unpleasant".

You may improve your self-esteem by being yourself when you get in touch with your feelings and when you voice them in an appropriate way.

BITE 16
ANGER.

This next section is devoted specifically to anger, since we are very bad at handling this emotion in the western culture.

Are you familiar with the expression "collecting stamps"? It means hiding your irritation at something or someone, rather than admitting it. You may think "getting irritated by a little thing like that is ridiculous" or "No, I don't want to quarrel now".

Not admitting what you feel will make you store up the emotions.

You might have said, I get irritated at this and that in a calm tone of voice, reacting straight away whenever you felt irritated. Instead a lot of emotions are stored up and after some time you will fly into a rage caused by some little thing at some point. Your reaction will be out of proportion and very difficult for some people around you to understand. This creates conflicts that are difficult to solve.

Now try instead to make a deal with the ones close to you about letting the others know whenever you get irritated. It need not be very detailed, only: "Now I feel irritated". It may even be a fun challenge to put it in words as soon as you feel it.

The rest of the family may react by answering, "Oh, do you want to tell me why?" or they can say nothing and just listen.

Please notice that you will no longer experience big clashes if you and your relatives are given the chance to express your irritation. You may even feel that fewer things are irritating you. After a month you may discuss what the exercise

showed you about anger and irritation.

BITE 17
STRESS

Most people suffering from stress have their own stories and the reasons for stress are individual.

However, stress always originates in the fear of not being able to meet the expectations of you held by yourself or your surroundings regardless of the expectations being realistic or unrealistic. On one hand there is positive stress like when you are in love. Gut pain, heart throbbing and sweaty hands may be some of the symptoms.

Some of the same symptoms accompany negative stress, although the pleasant feeling coming from the positive expectation of something agreeable is not present.

If you feel negative stress, it may be because you have to get better at opting out or at asking for help. Quite a lot of people fancy the idea of having to be perfect, they want to do everything better. However, they admit that they hold themselves to higher standards than they hold the people around them.

These sky-high and unrealistic expectations may begin in your childhood; however, it does not mean very much to your self-esteem when they began. What is important now is that you are an adult who can make decisions about, and understand, that you are doing well enough, doing your best and be satisfied with yourself.

How would you react if someone asked, "Would you please help me, I´m not sure I can handle this on my own?" Would you think he is weak and not good enough? Or would you think he was brave to ask for help and even tell him so?

Improving your self-esteem is really a good idea when you are working your way out of your stress. Among other things it is about being able to feel like yourself and to feel what is good for you. When you're able to feel what is good for you, you will also be able to feel what is not good for you.

Once you know yourself and the signals your body gives you when you're stressed, you can take them seriously and practice opting out or ask for help if something is difficult.

What would it be like saying, "I find this situation too stressful. I'll have to say no or get help!" and at the same time to have a good feeling in your gut? Try it now - get in touch with the feeling that it would be ok. Can you feel it? You can do it!

Stress occurs when you are not feeling sure of meeting your own expectations or those of other people. Sometimes we imagine that others expect something of us which is not true at all. Having a talk with them about your stress can relieve it.

MARGARET'S STORY

Margaret aged 37 started therapy due to a minor depression caused by stress. Margaret hadn't taken her stress seriously because she thought she was quite capable of managing everything herself. She found it very hard to recognize that it was an unreasonable expectation that she would manage everything, never complaining or opting out.

Margaret's 59–year-old mother made her come to her house twice a week to clean for her and prepare meals for the other days. Having done some shopping, cooked meals and cleaned the rooms, her mother's comment was that it was indeed the least one could expect. Margaret didn't feel that she did well enough, feeling irritated at the same time that she had to do so much for her mother. However, she never protested. She would feel terrible every time she snapped at her mother.

At work Margaret never said no to an assignment, worked late a lot and even allowed her colleagues' to interrupt her when she was talking. She made it a point of pride to perform well at work. But, in spite of always doing her best she never felt it was good enough. When being praised by her boss, she felt it was an indication that she could do even better.

Margaret was working herself to death. Everybody was expecting something of Margaret and she never opted out. The only one not allowed to expect anything of Margaret - was Margaret. In therapy Margaret started from scratch by getting in touch with herself, learning to feel if something was not good for her. It was a giant step for her when she could confront the mother, suggesting to her that she hire a cleaner.

Margaret did not want to live for others any more. She realized that it was ok living for oneself and it made her flourish. She realized that the energy to do something good to others increases when the idea comes from a good feeling.

BITE 18
LOW SELF-ESTEEM IN A RELATIONSHIP

Self-esteem plays an important part in our relationships with other people. It's important in all relationships, however, it's especially important in a serious romantic partnership, which is hopefully going to last a lifetime.

If you didn't grow up with a sense of your own intrinsic value, your sense of value will rely on external things: what you do or what you have. This will lead to a lot of discomfort, since you depend on the value that other people may attach to you. You will unconsciously search for a partner that will give you a sense of value.

During this process you may try to change yourself, because when you're in love you want to do anything to please your partner - even change your personality.

This will not last though. It means that you will do things or put up with things which you normally would not do. Gradually your capability to understand your own limits and needs will decrease, resulting in anger and a feeling of deserting yourself. This will cause you to become even more uncertain and sad.

JOAN and CAMERON'S STORY:

Joan and Cameron have begun therapy as they are losing interest in each other and their relationship. Cameron says that he gets very frustrated when he tells Joan he loves her and she doesn't reply straight away that she loves him too.

Joan replies that she feels irritated because it is as if Cameron is only using these words to get something back from her. Joan will say, "I love you", when feeling love, wanting to share it with Cameron.

Sometimes Joan feels that Cameron agrees with her or avoids disagreeing with her either in order to please her or to avoid a conflict.

Cameron considers this, agreeing with Joan´s supposition. Joan wants Cameron to be more honest, telling her what he needs and not being afraid of disagreeing.

It turns out that Cameron´s father acted the same way towards Cameron´s mother. Cameron realizes that this is a bad habit in their relationship and wants to break it with the help of Joan.

Some people find it easier to cope with their low self-esteem by having control of their surroundings either consciously or unconsciously. If you are in control of what happens the world becomes manageable and harmless and you can live with the feeling of not being good enough because you are in control of things nevertheless.

It may appear as a façade in which, everything is perfect, clean, new, smart, correct, expensive, big – everything to keep at a distance the fact that behind the façade you will find violent pain, emptiness and loneliness. It may also appear as a need to control the people around you.

However, that is a false feeling of safety, becoming destructive in the long term if people are controlled by means of fear. As the effect of fear decreases over time because we adapt to our experiences, the surroundings will again become impossible to control and you will have to increase the control, using stronger means.

From verbal threats of depriving someone of love, affection and community the control may become verbal humiliations and episodes of degradation and when this does not work either you may resort to physical violence to end the feeling of powerlessness.

PRISCILLA and JOSH'S STORY:

Priscilla and Josh start therapy because they find it difficult to talk to each other. Priscilla feels that Josh gets very angry and can even become threatening if she voices her dissatisfaction.

Josh agrees that he does have a temper, but after all he doesn't hit her. In his childhood home Josh saw that his father terrorized his mother and Josh swore that he would never become like that.

Until the couple starts therapy he has not been taught anything else and he relapses again and again into his old pattern, Priscilla becomes afraid of stopping him and opting out. Through therapy sessions Pricilla and Josh get the opportunity to learn new ways of communicating without Josh resorting to threats or Priscilla keeping things to herself out of fear.

I recommend individual therapy to Josh in order to clear up the past, but the couple choose to take up together the relevant issues since they have both skeletons in the closet.

They learn a new way of showing each other openness and confidence and together they set new goals for the future.

You get a false feeling of safety when people around you do as you tell them. Most of those exerting some kind of control are fully aware of what they are doing. They are aware that it is wrong and they apologize time and again for what they are doing. But since they have not been taught anything else, they cannot change their behavior and they cannot keep their promises. They themselves have got to recognize that they need help and must seek it out if this has to be changed.

The partner is rarely able to help. It takes professional help that can get to the root of the problems in an objective approach and deliver the tools necessary to change the pattern of action.

Likewise, the other side of the coin represents the partner who puts up with humiliation because of low self-esteem and who quite often comes from a home where humiliation and control are well known. Being creatures of habit we bring what is familiar to us to our grown-up lives, although it may not represent what's best for us. Familiarity creates a feeling of safety. We relate to it and a person that experienced humiliation during childhood will often choose a partner who can provide some kind of humiliation. If you fit one of these descriptions you cannot expect your partner to save you or to give you tools to change this.

BITE 19
SUPERDOG AND UNDERDOG

In some relationships one partner is dominating, making all the decisions. The other partner submits to this, accepting that the dominating one makes all the decisions. However, there is a price to be paid. First of all the superdog carries a great responsibility. Not only does the superdog make the decisions, by doing so the superdog accepts the responsibility for good or bad decisions.

The consequence is that the underdog can deny responsibility, blaming the superdog. "It happened because s/he wanted it. It might not have happened if s/he wasn´t always the one to decide." But what the underdog does not realize is that s/he carries as much responsibility for a decision because the underdog left it to the superdog. Leaving it to someone else to make decisions on one's behalf is also a choice. Therefore, the superdog is not the only one to blame.

Many superdogs are not aware of this pattern just like the underdogs rarely realize it, feeling victimized instead. The superdog feels frustrated, being reproached when something fails without being able to actually put a finger on the reason for it.

In a relationship it is fine for one partner to take over for the other during periods when the latter possesses less energy. It is ok when one partner has qualifications which are not shared by the other partner. But in the long view it is precarious for one partner to do all the decision making in the relationship.

Dealing with the finances for instance – in many relationships one of the partners is in charge of the finances. "I am innumerate, I don't get it". "She is so good at it, she sees to that". "I'm not interested, he takes care of that." If one of the partners share these attitudes, the person who is not in charge, can deny responsibility if anything goes wrong.

"Don't you have control of our finances? I thought you had our finances under control." "You must put our finances on a sound basis, I can't live with them being in a mess."

Denying one's responsibility in a certain area of the relationship is not always wrong but can create an imbalance, one partner having more power than the other. But the power may tilt, the moment the superdog is no longer in control or it does not work out according to the underdog´s opinion, the latter can turn on a dime and begin reproaching the superdog for the state of affairs. Now the superdog is made responsible for something the underdog accepted (silence gives consent) which is precarious.

In a healthy relationship one of the partners cannot accept being responsible for a certain area alone. Both must ensure that the other at least plays a part in the decisions that affect both partners.

Let's return to the example with the finances again: one partner can easily be responsible for having a good everyday grasp of the finances, seeing to it that the bills are paid. Once a month both partners need to go over the budget together. In this way they will both know which bills need to be paid, the balances of their accounts, of extraordinary expenses to be allowed for and of the amount to be saved.

Once in a while in my clinic I hear that one of the partners of a couple refuses responsibility for checking and updating the couples social calendar. Supporting each other in this way is of great value particularly when one of the partners is very busy on the job or goes through a crisis. However, when this becomes a permanent division of labour the couple will again find itself in a situation when the underdog opts out, avoiding showing any interest in any particular area.

In this way the underdog is pushed into the sidelines in the relationship so the underdog may later reproach the superdog "You know, I´m never asked if I want to come along." And the superdog may reproach the other partner for "not taking an interest in the family."

Sitting down on Sunday evenings to go over the plans for the next week is a possibility and decisions can be made to who will be making the phone calls and following up with this and that. This way the responsibility may be shared equally between the partners and the relationship may turn into a joint project.

The problem of underdog and superdog may also be found if one of the partners is verbally strong in contrast to the other. The partner with the best arguments for his/her view will carry his/her point, the other sulkily withdrawing or becoming sad.

BITE 20
DO YOU DARE TO SHOW YOUR TRUE SELF

Having low self-esteem makes it difficult for you to be your true self – even in an intimate relationship. "No, I'm not going to say anything about that in case he thinks I´m crazy". "I don't want to burden her with all my crap." "He is probably right so I´ll keep quiet."

One of the problems involved is that you will never show your partner your true self. How then is your partner to show you that s/he loves you body and soul? Not showing your partner your true self is being dishonest to your partner. Would you be able to live with her/him being dishonest to you?

What would it be like being loved for your absolute true self, your strong and weak points, good and bad, the whole lot? If you find this comforting you must give others a chance to see who you are.

Your background may include a pattern of dealing with the fact that there was no room for you, your emotions and what you contained as a child. Therefore, you probably learned that others do not want to see the whole of you. However, a sound relationship is built on honesty and openness and, therefore, you have to set out on the ice hoping that it will not break. Being loved for what the partner is expecting of you instead of what you really are is very dissatisfying.

I see quite a few people in my clinic because they have been living in a relationship under false pretences.

SOPHIA'S STORY:

Sophia begins therapy and recounts that her husband is forever praising her for being such a happy and cheerful person. "My Sophia never has an off-day!", and "Sophia really is my better half, she can make me feel happy even when I have a total off-day." Sophia attends therapy because she has stress and is slightly depressed. Her conscience is bothering her because she cannot live up to the picture of the happy and positive girl he fell for.

"If I am no longer the girl he fell for, will he want anything to do with me?"

Gradually, Sophia realizes that she has never actually told her partner that she also needs to be the little girl in need of help. That she experiences off-days without meaning as well and that behind her façade, feelings of guilt and sorrow are piling up that she never shows.

After a few sessions we invite her husband to join her at a therapy session. Sophia asks him about his reactions when she has always appeared strong and happy, and he answers that he likes that, but his conscience is bothering him at the same time. He feels that he is making too many demands on her, relying to heavily on Sophia´s ability to cheer him up when he is low-spirited.

Sometimes he also feels somewhat useless in the relationship because he feels that Sophia is having a difficult time. However, she always rejects him when he asks, telling him that nothing is wrong. This gives him the impression that she has no need of him. He feels left out and he doesn't know what to do.

His announcement takes Sophia by surprise and for a while we talk about Sophia´s hiding behind a façade. Being asked whether he would like to get to really know Sophia including her off-days, her sulkiness and other weak points, he sighs from the bottom of his heart saying he would like nothing better. It would make it much easier for him to help her when she is down, giving him a feeling that their relationship is more equal when he is allowed to experience one of her not very great days.

Sophia starts crying, deeply moved by his words. Her husband takes her by the hand saying, " It is ok, Sophia, I'm here with you;"at this point Sophia realizes that she has been misjudging her husband. Not only does he want the happy Sophia, he wants the real Sophia.

If you doubt whether your partner or others close to you really want to get to know your real self then ask them. It is by far the easiest way to find out. The worst thing that can happen is somebody refusing the offer, which will tell you which person not to open up for. This will help you to avoid disappointments. What would be your answer if one of those closest to you asked you the same question?

BITE 21
HOW TO GET RID OF YOUR LOW SELF-ESTEEM

Other people cannot help you to get rid of your low self-esteem by either praising, recognizing or encouraging you. Possessing low self-esteem is not changed by other people telling you how beautiful you are, how wise, fantastic or clever. Your self-esteem cannot be improved by other people, they can only give you a positive feeling which is short-lived – like a fix of self-esteem.

In the same way as our self-esteem is not improved by other people's applauding us, praising us and recognizing us, you yourself cannot improve your self-esteem by more knowledge, results at your job, material goods, marriage, children, charity work, sexual conquests or face lifts.

The work can only be carried out by being yourself.

This is a problem for many of us, since we were given no tools for this work when we left our homes, with the result that we haven't got the slightest idea of how to go about it.

Therefore, seeing a therapist may be a good idea as s/he knows some tools to pass on to you, which will make your work easier.

It's my sincere hope that this book will be of great help to you. Studying it industriously and working hard with the exercises can take you a long way in the right direction.

BITE 22
GO RIGHT AHEAD WITH IT - NOW

Many people intend to use displacement activities to avoid what they expect to be tiresome or difficult. Homework, cleaning, projects and many other things can be postponed by imagining that you just have to shop, telephone a friend, watch television, read emails or other activities.

Displacement activities may actually help you to unburden your head and gather strength for what you have to do. Working with self-esteem is different. Not one excuse can be found to postpone this work. "If only I had a better house/ a new fiancé/ a job that I liked better/ more time/ more money I would find energy to engage in the work." You may find excuses for postponing it because you are afraid of what will happen when you start working with your self-esteem. What old hurtful patterns will you come across? How will you change? What do you expect to feel obliged to change in your life as a result of the work?

Promise yourself that you will seek help if it proves too difficult for you – and then go right ahead.

BITE 23
AWARENESS

Try to recall the last time you did something that truly made you feel great while you work consciously with your emotions and how they work. Something that made you feel completely right and gave you a fantastic pleasant feeling. It need not be something big and you must not consider whether it was right or wrong to other people – only if it was right for you. It may take some time for you to recall when you last did something good for yourself so be patient.

If it's not possible for you to recall something good you did for yourself, you must find something good that you can do for you.

Close your eyes and recall the situation. Identify yourself with the situation again, recall or imagine what it feels like doing something good for yourself. Do you recognize your gut feeling? You must pay attention to that feeling as it will show you the way while you are improving your self-esteem.

Next time you experience doubts – anything - even small things, then close your eyes. Place your hand on your gut to experience the feeling. What does your gut tell you – what will make you experience this good feeling in your gut in a given situation? Chicken or meat balls? The red or the black blouse? Shall I stay or leave?

Your gut will always speak the truth, it will always tell you what you really wish and what is best for you. Acting according to it you will begin by taking yourself seriously, listening to yourself and supporting yourself.

Chicken or meatballs tonight for dinner may be the initial small questions before you soon go on to bigger issues: Is this job good for me? Is this relationship? Shall I say something now or refrain from it?

Here's the next step – when you take yourself seriously you will also find yourself in situations where you have to object and say no. There is no perfect way of doing it and you cannot avoid hurting someone or making others angry from time to time. That is part of life.

But you can practice objecting to something in a caring way by learning some of the techniques of effective communication. Make use of the exercises in the chapter on communication.

When you become good at recognizing your gut feelings and taking yourself seriously you will soon realize that stress for example doesn't have the same impact on you any longer. After some time, you see, you will automatically say no to things not good for you. Or you will realize that a tiresome task leads to an attractive goal, and the energy to make a smiling performance.

Even situations when your mind is buzzing and you're tossing and turning in bed will change because the answer lies in your gut, and listening to it those thoughts will no longer have the power to stir your mind in the same way as before.

TESS'S STORY:

I have a knack for falling in love with jerks who always put me on the back burner – their job, their hobbies or their children will always be first in line. I have always made excuses for them in the beginning of the relationship: "Well, this is so new that I can't really expect to be important from the beginning". Not until later when I realized that it would never change did I begin protesting – too late.

Finally I do realize that I choose and fall for superficial men but I have not been able to change it until I learned the exercise with my gut. I am still flirting with that kind of men but I quickly get the feeling of whether they are good for me or not.

I have become quite good at noticing my gut feeling when people are crossing the line and I've become good at objecting and stopping early.

I met a man recently who is not downgrading me in the same way, but what's more he wants to hear about my gut feelings and takes them very seriously. We discuss what may be wrong, and try to improve what is missing. I hardly dare to believe it, but my gut feeling tells me that I am on the right track.

Another way of creating awareness is to evaluate your everyday situations and feel them in a new way. Next time you are driving/eating/peeing/moving what does it feel like? Does it feel good to you? What's good about it? How can your body feel that it is good? Is something unpleasant or unlikeable? What does your body feel?

An example:

What does it feel like when I'm driving a car? It feels good and also scary.

What is nice about it? It is nice to get from one place to another and almost at my own pace. Where can I feel it? I feel it in my breast, it tingles, sensing the good feeling when I drive. What is scary about it is the big and heavy car that may kill both me and other people.

The unpleasant tingling in my solar plexus makes me feel that. This feeling increases in residential areas where children may be out playing.

The exercise is not meant to change your life drastically but to make you aware of how you feel much more directly and much more often. The habit of getting in touch with your gut feeling will gradually increase your own awareness of how you feel.

BITE 24

INTELLIGENCE AND SELF-ESTEEM

"Don't you have to be rather intelligent to work for a better self-esteem?" The person asking me that question was afraid she wasn't clever enough to achieve better self-esteem.

When working with your self-esteem emotional intelligence is what you need. There is no connection between IQ and emotional intelligence. You need not be wise to possess emotional intelligence. On the contrary, having a high IQ may sometimes pose a problem when working with self-esteem as you often become too intellectual about it, i.e. looking for logical explanations of everything in life and searching for rational solutions to problems. When working with your self-esteem you have to learn to trust your gut feeling.

If you're accustomed to a lot of "brain work" you may find that the concept of "gut feelings" is beyond your comfort zone. Intellectually you may "understand" the idea of self-esteem, but when it comes to gut feelings you will resist. Hopefully some of the exercises in the book may help you if your brain tries to get the upper hand while you are working with your self-esteem.

BITE 25
WORRIES

According to our cultural standards we imagine a responsible adult person to be someone who thinks and worries about things. If you don't worry about anything, you will be considered indifferent and indifference equals irresponsibility and none of us wants to be irresponsible.

But the bottom line is that worrying is rarely constructive and productive. You reach constructive and productive solutions as a result of your capability to think in constructive and productive ways NOT as a result of worrying.

Worries will fill your head without making any positive difference to you.

What would it be like to stop worrying? What would it feel like being without worries? Relieved? It would give you room and peace to find out whether there is a solution to the problem or not. If there is no solution you can spend your energy on accepting that which cannot be changed.

The human brain can only think of one thing at a time. So the answer to how to avoid worrying is rather simple – think of something else!

It may not seem quite so easy but it is pretty simple. You may think of reeling off the prime numbers in your head or focus on your breathing. If you focus on your breathing consciously and if you concentrate on focusing on it, you cannot think of anything else. Put what you are doing into words in your head: "I am taking a breath....I am exhaling air...."

Therefore, counting sheep makes for an excellent exercise if you cannot fall asleep because you're worrying. Imagine their wool, the grass and the fence they jump, what is behind them and all the details of the scenery. If your thoughts take you back to your worries, you just notice and return to your sheep. Worrying will make you tighten your muscles. You may not notice it but tension prevents you from finding rest and falling asleep. You may relax by cheating your brain with your sheep-counting and then you can fall asleep.

Worrying may sometimes be a defense mechanism against feeling. "I´m worried about what will happen if I speak my mind" may mean "I´m afraid of being hurt if I speak my mind".

Now try the following exercise:

Write down what worries you. Write down all you know about your worry, all possible angles on and solutions to the problem or consequences of not solving the problem. Then write down answers to the following questions without paying too much attention to a possible correct answer:

- ❖ What exactly does this problem mean to you right now?

- ❖ Is there anything I can do to change it right now?

- ❖ If I could do exactly what I wanted, I would…..

- ❖ What stops me from doing what I want?

- ❖ What can I do to change that?

BITE 26
LOW SPIRITS

Mostly low spirits will signal that you need to listen to yourself, that there is something you did or did not do. If you want not to repress the negative feelings or if you are going to a meeting where it is of greatest importance that you make a good impression – for example to a job interview, I have a tip for you:

Straighten your back, smile broadly, breathe deeply a few times and sing a happy song. (It doesn't matter what you sing, if only you sound happy when singing. "Happy Birthday" or "Twinkle, Twinkle, Little Star" are fine if those come to mind). If you try you may realize that it is physically impossible to be sad or angry, if you pretend you are happy.

Try to give it a thought – if you are generally a grumbler or dissatisfied most of the time, you will get even sadder and angrier by not trying to change. You yourself can change and so can your life with this little trick and you can program yourself to become happier. Don't use the trick too much though. It IS a trick and if you continuously use a trick to look happy, you will be inauthentic to yourself and your self-esteem will suffer. Use it only where needed.

The way you communicate influences your spirits remarkably and the way other people see you as well.

You can read further about this in the chapter on communication.

BITE 27
WHAT IS THE WORST THAT CAN HAPPEN?

Ask yourself that question: "What is the worst that can happen?"

Ask the question now and every time you face a challenge or a problem, big or small.

Having fully realized what would be by far the worst scenario for you, then try to find out if something may be changed or it is impossible to change anything. In case nothing can be changed then accept the state of affairs and do everything necessary to look after yourself. You can accept it by closing your eyes and picturing what it would feel like in your body if you accepted it. When you can feel acceptance, speak it out loud: "I accept that I cannot change this!"

Kathy says, Asking myself that question made a huge difference. I found out that the worst that can happen really isn't so bad. I can feel my tensions and worries disappear.

BITE 28
WHO AM I REALLY?

Do you really know yourself? Do you know which qualities you have? In order for other people to get to know you and in order that you will know whether they speak the truth when talking about you, you must get to know yourself.

Below you will find an exercise that may help you to get to know yourself better and to go on working with yourself.

Put a check beside all the qualities you have shown or used just once in your life. For example, you may tick off "patient" even if you have only been patient once in your lifetime.

- ❖ Loving

- ❖ Honest

- ❖ Loyal

- ❖ Impressionable

- ❖ Compassionate

- ❖ Patient

- ❖ Energetic

- ❖ Enterprising

- ❖ Spontaneous

- ❖ Funny

- ❖ Wise

- ❖ Helpful

- ❖ Categorical

- ❖ Understanding

- ❖ Open minded

- ❖ Curious

- ❖ Inventive

- ❖ Good at setting boundaries

- ❖ Diplomatic

- ❖ Embracing

- ❖ Warm

- ❖ Ambitious

- ❖ Friendly

- ❖ Lively

What is exciting about this exercise is that you can only check a quality that you already possess!. It means that all the qualities that you checked already form part of you. It may be a long time since you used the quality in question, but you can easily say, "I'm a spontaneous person," if only you were just once in your life, because you do have the ability to be spontaneous.

Now that you're familiar with the qualities you possess, it is up to you to use them whenever you want to. Which qualities would you like to use more? Think of what you can do to use a certain quality that you like. It certainly does not have to be world something world-shaking: bake a cake for someone with a sweet tooth, smile at an irritated store clerk or do something else that typifies the quality you want to make more use of.

In addition try to check off the qualities that are possessed by a good human being. Do they coincide with your own qualities? Imagine what it feels like being a good human being? Feel your gut – if you recognize the feeling, you have the good human being in you. Can you feel it? What does it feel like? Is it a nice feeling? Tell somebody you know about the exercise and about the feeling you got when you discovered something good about yourself!

BITE 29
PLANNING FOR CHANGES

When you plan to work to improve your self-esteem you have to keep a few things in mind. You have to do things you don't normally do and to recognize that you are capable of more than you imagine. To many people this will mean stepping far outside their comfort zone and that is why you should start small.

When you are in bed tonight try to think of the things you are going to do tomorrow. Will any of it be influenced by your self-esteem and can you change any without great consequences?

One of my clients referred to the above: "There is a very nice girl at the check–out at the local supermarket, I really wish I could pluck up my courage to smile at her and say, "Hello." Instead I keep looking at the floor and just pay without saying anything."

The following day when he went shopping, he decided that he would look her straight in the eye, giving her a smile. In case he could cope, he would add "Hello."

What he had to consider – and that goes for you as well – what is the worst that may happen? He said that the worst that could happen to him was that he might blush deeply and that she would find him ridiculous. I asked him to consider the effect of that and he answered that he would be both embarrassed and ashamed. I asked him to consider if anything worse would actually happen in that case. He did not think so. I asked him to feel what it would be like when he felt embarrassed and ashamed, probing to find out whether he would be able to stand that feeling. We worked a little with it until he found he could stand it if the worst happened.

I suggested to him that he should give it a try when he felt ready. The following week he came to see me:

The day after my last session I was fully determined to give her a smile. But when I entered the supermarket she was not there at all. The following day I went there again and there she was, but I did not have the time to smile at her so I got embarrassed, blushing deeply so I had to look down. I got so angry with myself at it that I decided to give her a smile at all costs the next day.

And I did so. I gave her a smile, a somewhat silly smile and she looked at me – and then she smiled back. And do you know what happened? She was the one to blush. Then I smiled even more at her so that she could see that she shouldn't feel ashamed for blushing. It was so cool! Two days later I was in the supermarket again, giving her a smile again, and she smiled back. I said "Hello", which she returned. It was really nice and I felt proud that I had broken the ice."

Some people will find such an exercise too daunting and for others it will be smooth sailing. You have to find something that will push your limits, but not to a degree that will prevent you from trying. You might try refusing a task you have no time for, telling your partner what you want, signing up for a course, that you never dared to do before, or telling another person about yourself. Find something manageable which will make you proud of doing at the same time and go ahead with planning when and how to do it.

BITE 30

SPONTANEOUS ANSWERING – LEARN TO FOLLOW YOUR INTUITION

Try to answer the following questions quickly without reflecting on what the best answer would be:

If I allowed myself to say no when I mean no, what would then be the positive out-come for me?

If I allowed myself to say yes when I mean yes, what would be the positive out-come for me?

If I was not to live up to other people's expectations of me what would be the positive out-come for me?

If I was not scared at all what would I do right now?

Sometimes you give the best answers by answering quickly without reflecting. Taking your time to answer you may begin to reflect on the pros and cons depriving yourself of the possibility to brainstorm with yourself. This exercise may reveal to you the advantages that go with an improved self-esteem which may be a motivator for you.

BITE 31
WRITE A DIARY ON YOUR SUCCESSES

Every evening you can make an entry in a notebook that contains your successful accomplishments of the day. You may write as much as you are capable of, it need not be extensive, taking a lot of time, a few simple words will certainly do.

An example from an entry: "Rejected a task because of lack of time" or "Told my Mother that I´ll call her on Sunday, asking her not to call me until then. She got sad but I stuck to it."

If you have the time, you may write about some of the changes or the new initiatives you are planning to carry out – however, it is important not to overburden yourself with too many or too big tasks. Make it practical and you are bound to succeed and with one or more small successes in the bag you are ready to face bigger challenges. Do not plan more than one or two tasks at a time and no further ahead than a week until you have experienced successes, which makes you feel it is fine to bite off bigger pieces.

Remember to make specific notes on what you did which will later be useful as reminders and motivators.

Overweight persons may make the mistake of planning to lose 20 pounds all at once. That project will take an incredibly long time. Perhaps you have already tried and failed to do this, and you know that the "pat on your back" to recognize your good work is too far out in the future. Try instead to plan to lose 5 pounds which is a more attainable goal and you can praise yourself sooner for this success. And, having having met your smaller goal, you will automatically feel greater motivation to go on. The next project might then be to stick to your new weight for 2 months, then plan to lose 5 additional pounds and so on.

Use this model to plan your changes, it is better to make several minor changes in the beginning because this will improve your chances of success. Write successful entries in your diary regardless of how small they seem.

BITE 32
PIECES OF GOOD ADVICE

Here's some pieces of good advice to be put up on your refrigerator for inspiration:

- Think of what makes you happy (you know the feeling of feel-good in your gut) which you like and then make yourself happy pretty often.

- Draw up a list that shows the things you are good at and the things you do well. Start with minor things like "I´m really good at making coffee" or "I'm an excellent driver", add others as you think of them. Think of what you are good at in your everyday life and add this to the list.

- You have got to be honest more often when being asked "How are you?" instead of saying, "I'm fine, thank you!" Sum it up in short sentences like "You know, I'm working with my self-esteem which is hard", or "I feel I make progress working with my self-esteem, which is very nice."

- When you are praised by others you will thank them instead of contradicting them. When you are praised it is because others see you that way, which is well within their rights. You need not fail to appreciate their estimation of you.

- If you do something foolish go ahead and apologize. Everybody makes mistakes so the idea is not to avoid making mistakes but to accept that you make mistakes from time to time and that's ok. If you yourself accept making mistakes, others will usually do it as well, forgiving your mistakes. But most important of all: forgive yourself for making mistakes. Try to say," I forgive myself for making that mistake." Be honest about forgiving yourself, then find your good gut feeling.

BITE 33
FOOD AND EXERCISE

You are in the middle of a mental process which takes time. Attending well to your body will help you feel a difference. It might be a long and sometimes difficult process to get in the habit of if you are not used to taking good care of your body. Doing it bit by bit will give you successes along the way.

Cut down on sugar and caffeine. Eat more fresh fruit and vegetables, preferably organic. Get a good night's sleep, and find out what you have to change to get a good night's sleep if you don't. Exercise, a daily walk or jog works wonders because your body will then produce the materials necessary for your good spirits and your energy. Try parking your car at a distance from your work and then walk the rest of the way. Or take a jog after dinner and the news. Do not drink alcohol more than once a week.

The Internet is full of great advice about eating healthfully and exercising, so I won't go into any more detail about that in this book. Just remember to take small steps, change one little thing, so that your lifestyle changes does not overwhelm you. Take time for them to turn into good habits. For example - change your breakfast routine and let that be the only change for 6 weeks, then take the next step. That way your lifestyle changes has time to become habits and your chance of success will be much greater!

BITE 34
AVOID BEING ISOLATED

When you're feeling bad you may react by withdrawing from other people which is quite natural. But it may not be the most appropriate way to handle things, because isolation will make your thoughts go round in circles, taking up more space than needed. Indeed isolation may make you even sadder and more worried.

You need not be a party animal, however, it is good for you to make room in your calendar for social activities once or twice a week. Preferably with people whom you trust and with whom you can share your experiences in regard your work with higher self-esteem. Spending time with your kids does not qualify as social time, nor is it appropriate to share your process with them unless they are adults and specifically answers yes when asked directly. The reason for this is the danger of overstepping your children's boundaries which is something that happens in a lot of families with low self-esteem.

Ian says, "I signed up for an evening class. The first five times I didn't say anything, I just sat there feeling stupid and alone.. Then I plucked up my courage, asking if anyone would join me for a beer. Some were happy to do so. Today one of them is my best friend and we can talk about everything."

BITE 35
ACCEPTING HELP

In my practice some of my clients will often say, "Sometimes I make it difficult for others to give me what I need."

Making it difficult for others to help comes in various ways:

- ❖ when you don't tell them what you want

- ❖ when you pretend that you don't need anything

- ❖ when you pretend to be completely self-sufficient

- ❖ when you ridicule others´ attempts to help you

- ❖ when you keep on giving and by doing so keep others at a distance

- ❖ when you seem "distant", not being present mentally

- ❖ when you are criticizing

- ❖ when you will not even allow yourself to find out what you want

It all stops you from showing others who your true self really is. It may be because you are afraid of letting them see your true self. It may be a way for low self-esteem to make itself felt.

If you recognize the above, try to write down examples of your doing so. What could have been done instead? At the worst what would have happened if you had said what you needed?

What do you give up when you are afraid of being rejected/ridiculed/hurt? It makes for a vicious cycle: you not saying what you need and then not having it which frustrates you so you feel your low self-esteem and keep silent about what you need.

You could turn it into a good cycle by asking for what you need, by doing so there is a much bigger chance of your getting what you need. This makes you happy and makes you feel important, and you improve your self-esteem, learning the value of asking for what you need.

BITE 36
SHARING YOUR EXPERIENCES

Once you have started working on your self-esteem it will be worthwhile to share your thoughts and experiences with others. You may not be used to being open with others and may doubt whether they can be trusted. If you do not know who to trust, there is only one way to find out – give it a try and see what happens.

If you know a person that will support you tell him that you have this book and have started studying it in order to improve your self-esteem. Be brief and precise. Then let the person support you as much as s/he can.

If you do not know a trustworthy person or you are uncertain about whom to trust, then choose the person you find to be the least "dangerous", for example a colleague at your job with whom you agree on many occasions. Tell them the above and experience the support and/or interest you get from them.

Accept it, don't contradict them, if they praise you for your efforts – you deserve it! Try to take a deep breath and feel the joy of being recognized for a job well done.

The very best for you would be to find a few colleagues or friends who will read the book too and meet you every second week to discuss changes, challenges and experiences. Personal development will always move faster if you are in a group; so if you can bring together a small group, it will be worth your while.

BITE 37
COMMUNICATION

You may think: What is the purpose of a chapter on communication in a book on self-esteem?

However, when working with self-esteem it is of great importance how you express yourself. Our brains will pick up various shades of the spoken language. Therefore, the choice of words and the stressing of the individual words constitute both the meaning of your message and how it is received by the person you are communicating with.

Many people have a tendency to use "one" or "you" instead of "I" when they are asked to describe themselves or talk about how they are. It seems to be a kind of cultural fear of contact typical in our part of the world which it will be worthwhile to avoid.

Instead of saying, "You'd want a partner who truly loves you", try to say, "I want be loved, I deserve to be loved, I like to be loved".

Be aware of it in your everyday life, try to change it by using "I" instead of "one" or "you".

BITE 38
IMPROVE THE WAY YOU EXPRESS YOURSELF

The way you speak – both to yourself and others – is of great importance. As mentioned earlier we define ourselves as human beings by what we are, what we do and what we have. We need to be aware of the power of words when speaking about ourselves or about others.

First and foremost you may focus on becoming aware of how you talk about yourself and others.

Here's some examples of what you may say about yourself or others:

- ❖ I'm stupid

- ❖ He's an idiot

- ❖ She is impossible

- ❖ I'm not good at it

- ❖ She's bad at it

- ❖ He is a problem/he's no good

- ❖ She is dominating

I'm sure you can come up with many more examples. All these statements say something about how a person is, and the problem here is that we can't change who we are but only what we do. So telling a story about how you or others are leaves you no possibilities to change it.

However, changing the statements into expressions describing actions, leaves you the possibility to improve your statements:

- ❖ I'm stupid becomes: "I feel stupid for doing that"

- ❖ He is an idiot becomes: "I don't think he quite understands what is needed"

- ❖ She is impossible becomes: "That wasn't very well done"

- ❖ I'm not good at it becomes: "I didn't do well enough"

- ❖ She is bad at it becomes: "She's not doing it quite right"

- ❖ He is a problem/he's no good becomes: "He doesn't always do what is most suitable"

- ❖ She is dominating becomes: "She really wanted to be in charge in that situation"

Making your expressions more forward-looking will make them appear less definitive:

I´m stupid becomes: "I feel stupid for doing that", which again turns into: "I'll do better next time"

Now you have not stigmatized yourself as stupid, instead you are looking forward, your language signals belief in and room for improvement. You may feel stupid for a time but have faith that this feeling is temporary. Believe it or not the choice of words and the stressing of them do matter.

I hope you can see the point of this exercise, as it is of great importance. It's not only about you and the way you talk about yourself but it deals with the signals you are sending to the surrounding world. Your signals tell others that you understand them, you have a mental room for them without judging them and you are not going to reject them. Getting used to "speaking with self-esteem" will attract other people doing the same and with whom you can talk frankly about everything and whom you can trust.

BITE 39

FEELING HURT

When you talk to other people and they answer back, this may hurt you although they didn't mean to. Making it clear that the responsibility for feeling hurt lies with you, try to tell them the following: "I was a bit hurt by that, did you intend that?"

How often do you think you will get a positive answer? The number of people saying things to hurt others on purpose are fewer than those dying from drowning in whipped cream! If you point this out, most people will be helpful and the feeling of being hurt pass away.

By telling others about what happens inside you, you take responsibility for yourself.

By telling others frankly how you are, you give them the chance to help and support you.

Opening yourself to others will cause some of them to open up to you as well.

BITE 40
WHEN ANOTHER PERSON'S PERSONALITY PROVOKES YOU

Do you know the feeling? You meet someone who does something that makes you irritated? It could be a person who speaks very loudly, always speaks his mind,, never says a word, laughs in a certain way, brags about his possessions, speaks in straightforward terms, avoids conflicts, loves conflicts – basically any action can trigger the "annoyance button" with someone.

The experience of being provoked by someone's actions may be caused by your dislike of a possible resemblance to the person. If you're outraged by certain people's actions it is most likely the very quality within yourself you do not like.

During therapy sessions John says that he cannot stand people who cannot get along. "How hard can it possibly be", he says, "Why not talk about it! I see no reason to discuss disagreements and certainly not when others are present. Disagreements belong to the private sphere.

When I dig into the things provoking his irritation, it becomes evident that John is the one to pour oil on troubled waters when the family disagrees. He finds conflicts difficult and gets really mad himself, he has to remove himself physically from the situation.

It turns out that John´s father was like that too and that throughout his life John has been working not to be like his father. It is a major defeat for him to realize that he cannot avoid being his father's son. Realizing this gives him a kind of "aha" experience. He asks, "Does that mean that I simply have to accept disagreements around me without feeling responsible for them? You know, this will make things much easier!"

BITE 41
WILL HEALTHY SELF-ESTEEM MAKE ME ANOTHER PERSON?

Fear of changes may keep us from doing what is best for us.

"If I improve my self-esteem, will I have to get a divorce and quit my job?" This was asked by one of my clients who decided to work with his self-esteem. He did not feel good about himself, however, the way he felt was safe and well known. He suffered from depression, conflicts that messed up his relationships and a boss that expected him to be at his job around the clock for the sake of the company. Your life may not look that bad, but you may fear the changes that may occur in you.

Sometimes in the process you may experience a certain confusion and doubt that you are on the right track. When you feel like this you should try to accept that feeling, then search for your gut feeling to learn what will be right for you.

Your friends may start wondering why you accept or reject proposals or why you have started talking about your emotions, telling them about your gut feeling. It may separate you for a time or it may inspire them to look into the possibility of improving their self-esteem. We all share a built-in resistance to change - some feel it stronger than others. You cannot fight it and expect it to die. But you can accept it as part of yourself, deciding that it will not rule you because you see the advantages of healthier self-esteem.

You chose your partner on the basis of your qualifications at that time. When you develop into a human being with self-esteem, most people will enjoy it, feeling happy together with you.

If they cannot, it is not your problem. You have no obligation to depend on an unhappy life. If you are honest with yourself, and with your partner, the right partner will love you for what you are and for who you are. Not for what you were once, leading a miserable life.

Gaining more self-confidence, openness, spontaneity, happiness and radiating self-respect may confuse other people. They may either change their behavior suiting their behavior to your new ones, or they may try to push you back into your old pattern.

Casting doubt on or even degrading your newly acquired and consequently frail self-esteem is not exactly what you are looking for. You need people like yourself who want to improve their lives. It's ok to accept the fact that you have a right to a life with happiness and that you deserve it.

BITE 42
FINAL COMMENTS

I want you to embrace the wonderful, difficult and fantastic challenge it is to work with your self-esteem. I hope the book provided you with new insight, at the same time clarifying lots of things with which you are already familiar, making it easier for you to stick to your decision.

I grew up in a family with an alcoholic mother and a narcissistic father in a neighbourhood with a lot of dysfunctional families, so the issue of self-esteem has been very present in my life. I have worked through it. I feel my low self-esteem from time to time, but it neither scares me nor rules me. I look it in the eye, acknowledge that it is there and then ignore it, living my life the way I think it should be lived.

I hope that the book has enabled you to look at yourself and others in a new and broader light.

I hope that you will see far more opportunities than limitations.

I have no doubt that you will succeed – all the best along the way!

A Note From the Author

Should you feel the need to give feedback on the book or let me know how it helped you, you are more than welcome to contact me by email to connect@visiblehearts.com or on my English Facebook page https://www.facebook.com/BeingMariah/ - I can't guarantee that you will get an answer, but I read all the emails I get!

Acknowledgements

I want to thank all the people who made it possible for me to write this book. There are many - and whether they spent hours or days on the book or on debating the contents of the book with me, they all made a huge difference. My gratitude go to my family, friends, clients, colleagues, fellow students and teachers - because everyone I met on my way through life contributed to the book.

Thanks to the people who provided feedback, corrected my poor punctuation, inappropriate language errors, gave me "food for thought" and inspired me to formulate understandable explanations.

Mariah Wolfe

Born 1966 in Denmark.

Qualified psychotherapist, couple's therapist and speaker.

Self-employed, practice online through online courses, phone and Zoom.
Read more on www.visiblehearts.com

Previously written books

Selvværd for begyndere (The Power To Be You)

Gnist, Nærvær og Samtale (Not published in English)

Poul Glargaards datter (Not published in English)

Helterejsen (Your Hero's Journey. Published 2014)

Dead Men, a serial killer thriller, (Published 2015)

How to handle the classic narcissist - in families, in relationships, and in the workplace (Published 2019)